ADA

ADA

Journey of a Post Slavery Negro Woman of Valor

DOLORES M. LOTT

iUniverse, Inc.
Bloomington

Ada
Journey of a Post Slavery Negro Woman of Valor

iUniverse books may be ordered through booksellers or by contacting:

iUniverse
1663 Liberty Drive
Bloomington, IN 47403
www.iuniverse.com
1-800-Authors (1-800-288-4677)

ISBN: 978-1-4759-2231-8 (sc)
ISBN: 978-1-4759-2232-5 (hc)
ISBN: 978-1-4759-2233-2 (ebk)

Printed in the United States of America

iUniverse rev. date: 05/24/2012

CONTENTS

CHAPTER 1

The Sunset

The September 27, 1979 local weekly news journal called the Register gave this front page account: **Final Rites Held for Mrs. Ada Woods**—Mrs. Ada Woods, 83, of 2007 Wyoming Street died of a heart attack on Thursday, September 13. Widow of the late Isaac Woods of Rockdale, Texas, she was the fourth child of twelve born to the late Champ and Isabel green of Lexington, Texas, where she attended school and at an early age professed her faith in Christ. Mrs. Woods had resided in San Antonio for the past 46 years.

She was a faithful member of the Greater Corinth Baptist Church where she served under the leadership of the late Reverend W.B. Myers, J.H. Hardeman and the present pastor—Reverend B. Tyree Alexander—on Usher Board No. 1 and the Ladies Aide Society until her health failed her. She was also a member of the American Legion Auxiliary 828, Fred Brock Unit.

Although the mother of only one daughter, Mrs. Woods had been a voluntary foster parent for countless numbers of young people both relatives and strangers who found their way to her door, who shared her love and called her "mama".

She is survived by: Daughter and son-in-law, Dolores Maxine and Rufus Lott; grandchildren—Andrea Lynn White, Frank White III, Rufus Jr.,Vernon, David, Lorenzo, Fred and Maxine Lott; great-grand children—Sharreffia and Lynette Lewis, Fred, Jabar and Goldie Lott; niece and grand niece Laura Bell Washington and Laura Jamison; six nephews, six nieces and six great-grand nieces of Houston, San Antonio, Corpus

Christ and Lexington Texas and San Francisco California; and a host of cousins in the San Antonio and Lee County Areas.

The Genesis

It seemed to be a normal day in the Green household. Isabel was in the kitchen making bread for her family. This was a daily morning chore for the tall attractive biracial mother—victim of miscegenation. Her parents were Ceasar and Eliza Journer. Her biological father was slave master Smith, who sired two daughters by Eliza. These two daughters had very fair complexion and very long naturally wavy hair. But Eliza and her husband, Ceasar, had other children who were medium to very dark-skinned with kinky hair. Eliza, attempting to prevent envy among her dark-skinned daughters, cut the two biracial daughters' hair to just below the ear. It appeared the gesture solved what she thought would be a problem.

In this small town of Lexington, Texas in 1884, Champ Green moved his family from the country farm to this promising town boasting a population of 250, but doubling to over 500 shortly after the arrival of the San Antonio and Aransas Pass Railroad in 1890,

The children—Bud the eldest, Bertha and Della had been extremely excited about the move into town. They could go to school nearby and have friends. As they talked about things to happen, Isabel entered in the room and said in a very calm manner, "Children I need you to go down to Mrs. Lewis' house and tell her you've come to do whatever she needs for you to do. And tell her I'm ready." Bud seemed completely stunned by this request, but Bertha and Della knew what was about to happen. Isabel looked sternly at Bertha and said, "Bertha be sure and take care of Mrs. Lewis' babies. Fix some food because she might be here for a while." Looking pensively at her mother, Bertha said, "Yes ma'am, and I'll make Bud play with the boys. Now Bertha was almost 6 years old and Della 4, but these little girls had learned much from their mother in taking care of the home and the preparation of food. And so, they could do many household chores that other children of their same age could not. Isabel is lauded by neighbors for her on-the-job training of her children. No one had the privilege to be idle in her house when things needed to be done.

On the way to Mrs. Lewis' house Bud asked, "Della why is mama sending us to Mrs. Lewis' house to do work there when we have chores to do at home? And you know Papa is going to be upset if I haven't planted the collard greens, cabbage, corn and potatoes 'cause you know me and papa plowed the ground yesterday evening so I could plant today. You know he's gonna be mad."

Now although Bud was the oldest child, it was evident that there was quite a difference in his mental age and his chronological age. It was accepted that although he would grow and develop into a robust, handsome man, mentally he would remain a child.

The girls looked at each other and smiled, because they knew what was about to happen when Mrs. Lewis made it to their house. And Bertha said, "Bud, don't worry, I'm pretty sure Papa won't be mad about you not getting the collard greens and okra planted when he gets home. He'll have something to take his mind off everything for awhile." Bud was quite comfortable now because Bertha always told him the truth.

When Mrs. Lewis entered the house and saw Isabel cooking in the kitchen, she was upset and with a stern voice said, "Isabel! What are you doing? I can see you're having pain. How close are they?" Having prepared a complete dinner of smothered rabbit, collard greens, baked sweet potatoes, rice and corn bread, she looked at Mrs. Lewis, smiled and said, "Old friend, it's time."

The old friend served as the midwife for the birth of Isabel's fourth child. It took a while with excruciating labor pains before a tiny baby girl arrived kicking and screaming. Isabel couldn't believe how small she was causing unprecedented pain compared to the three other children who had long torsos, long arms and legs at birth and it was evident by their growth cycle they would be tall children, teenagers and adults.

Mrs. Lewis, in addition to serving as an effective midwife, cleaned up the delivery area and the newborn, dressed her, put her in Isabel's arms and checked on the food Isabel had prepared. As she was leaving she told Isabel to send one of the children for her if she was having any problem and she would come back. She said, "That little girl is a beauty, and I predict she is going to be a feisty one to cope with" as she laughed.

When she arrived at home, Mrs. Lewis found her own children under control. Bertha and Della had prepared ham sandwiches and lemonade for them, and Bud had kept the little boys entertained. Mrs. Lewis, smiling, thanked them and told them that their mother had a big surprise for them. Bud was the first to run out the door, down the road, to the house. The girls followed just as eager. As the three hurried in the house,

Isabel was not in the kitchen as they expected, Bud that is. The girls knew to go to the bedroom. And so, Bud followed. They saw their mother in bed. Bertha was the first to say, "Are you alright mama?" Nodding in the affirmative, smiling and shifting her eyes to the little bundle she had in her arms, she said, "Children you have a little sister." Bud rushed to the side to see this new life, and looking at the sleeping epitome of a doll, Bud excited said, "Mama she's 'purity,' can I play with her?" And Isabel, as kind as she could replied, "In a few days Bud; she needs to get a little bigger." Accepting his mother's explanation, he asked, "What's her name?" "I think we need to wait until your father comes to be a part of what her name's going to be." The girls were told to set the table for dinner, and Bud was told to go and feed the chickens. Reluctantly he left, but soon returned as if he had to watch over this newborn as did the girls who also returned to the bedroom.

Hearing the buggy wheels and trot of the horse, they knew their father was about to enter, and they were anxious to see his reaction to the newcomer.

Champ Green, their father, whose statue and appearance would cause one to believe he was a descendent of the African Bushman tribe. He was about 5 ft. 5, 150 pounds, a dark complexioned man who moved with swiftness all the time. As he entered the house from the back door, despite the smell of the well-prepared dinner, he sensed something had happened in the house. Della, the youngest, and Bud rushed to him, and with a great deal of emotion Della said, "Papa, come see what the stark brought mama." Bud was afraid to say anything because he knew his father was going to be upset because he hadn't done anything he had been told to do that day. Taking Champ by the hand, Della pulled him into the bedroom as if he didn't know the way. Champ was surprised indeed to see Isabel in bed with a new born that he thought was not due for another month. Moving quickly, he went over to Isabel, leaned over and kissed her and asked her if she was all right and if she needed anything. Her reply was "No, I'm fine, the baby is fine and Mrs. Lewis was a great help." But the excitement took on a new height as Champ came around the bedside to see his new daughter. As he looked at this tiny babe, he immediately developed an affinity for this one unlike the previous three. She was beautiful in his sight. He knew she was going to be different in statue. She did not have the long legs and arms, the pale complexion, but she was petite with what he declared later as 'tea cake tan' complexion. She was never going to be as dark skinned as Bud nor as light skinned as Isabel and the two older girls. And so on this memorable day of February 26, 1895 and the fourth child's birth, Champ felt it necessary to do something he hadn't done before. He picked up this tiny vessel, caressed her and kissed her. When he felt her squirming, he handed her back to Isabel, who began breast feeding her. "What'cha gonna name her?" Bud asked. He realized he had not been scolded by his father. Champ looked at Bud sternly and said, "So this is why you didn't do the planting I told you to do this morning?" Fearful of what this pint-size man would do next, Bud put his head down and said, "Yes suh, Papa, but . . . ." Interrupting him and putting his hand on Bud's shoulder to which Bud shook, Champ said, "It's okay son. You can get up early in the morning and do it." Bud was relieved and grateful, and said, "Yes suh Papa." "Now about that name, what do you think Isabel?" Champ asked. A moment of silence occurred before Isabel said in a somewhat restrained manner, "We should name her Vissey after your mother. As Champ thought about his slave mother, whom he loved, he thought about the fact that all her friends and her neighbors believed that she saw spirits, and he did not want this stigma on this newborn. So he said, "I think she needs an independent name." "What do you think about Louisa," he said. No one was going to have a controversial idea about what Champ suggested. So they all agreed that was a great name.

Isabel instructed them that it was dinnertime. They should all go to the kitchen, say a blessing for the food and especially for Louisa—the newborn. By the aroma that permeated the house, they all knew, despite her condition, Isabel had cooked a great meal. And despite her rather painful condition, Isabel joined them at the kitchen table with Louisa in her arms.

The Name Change

Now Louisa, the central figure of her siblings, understood at age four she was the apple of her father's eyes. So, on her fourth birthday she said to Champ, "Papa, I don't like my name; I want to change it. He and everybody who heard this preposterous request laughed out loud. But Louisa didn't laugh, and to emphasize her demand she said, "I want my name to be Ada." There was silence with everybody waiting to hear what Champ was going to say. What he wanted to do was pick her up, cuddle her, and tell her that it couldn't be done. But, when he looked at those big brown eyes and the seriousness in her countenance, he looked at Isabel who smiled and said to Champ's dismay, "I think that's a great idea." But she added, "I don't think there are any others who want to change their name." There was a resounding, "no sir" from the girls and an emphatic "no suh" from Bud. And Champ, speaking to the demanding little four-year-old, said, "Well, you and I will have to go to the Lee County seat Friday afternoon and get this change made." It was discerned by the rest of the children that this little girl had a special commanding force about her that their father couldn't resist.

The following Christmas, for example, Champ placed under the Christmas tree after all the children had gone to bed dolls for the girls. They were pretty white dolls with blond hair—the only complexion of dolls available in the small German town in the 1890's. But Ada didn't like her doll and ordered vociferously, "Papa, I don't want this doll with this 'yellow hair'. I want another one with black hair. It was apparent at this early stage of her life, she recognized the racial difference in complexion and hair of the people she saw in this small community of Lexington, Texas whose Caucasian population was mostly of German descent. As was done with the name change, the day after Christmas, Champ went back to Sam People's Dry Good Store in the small downtown area and changed the doll. It was evident this very small creature was becoming a dominant figure to deal with in Champ Green's household. Isabel found it fascinating, but did in no way make her feelings known.

CHAPTER 2

The Family Expansion

Although Louisa now changed to Ada was truly her father's love, the family did not end with her. For over the next 17 years came Mollie, Lena /short for Paulina/, twin boys Fate and Minor, Cissie, Ollie, Onnie and Fannie.

Now when the twins were born, Isabel was alone. She struggled with the birthing and did a perfect job of cleaning up and doing all that she was required to do for the new born healthy twin boys who were not identical in any since of the word. It was evident that Fate would be tall and thin and Minor would be short and stocky. When Champ and the children came home from working on the farm, they were at awe at what they saw. They all knew a baby was coming soon, but no one knew that this addition to the family would be twins.

Isabel became very ill as a result of all that she did and was bedridden for several days. Even Champ was afraid about Isabel's failing health condition, and constantly prayed for healing, which was an unusual act for Champ. But even in her frail condition, Isabel was able to mandate house chores be done and the outhouse be maintained. Well water was used to clean the 'slop jar' which was a ten-gallon bucket with a handle that was used inside the house at night for family elimination necessity.

She instructed Bertha and Della what to prepare for their meals. And Bud's job was to cut enough firewood for the pot-belly stove in the kitchen for meal preparation and the fire place that kept most of the house heated.

CHAPTER 3

Living Means

Now Champ had worked very hard on the farm that year to have enough vegetables and fruits to sell to the town merchants. He had engaged one of Mrs. Lewis' sons along with Bud to assist him in the planting and harvesting process. Of course Bud still had the responsibility of maintaining the garden at the house. He did have the wherewithal to teach his little twin brothers to do some minor things to help him. One might say that Bud did have a talent, and that was a green thumb.

In addition to the resources gained from their vegetables and fruit sales, Champ and his three older children during the summer months prior to Christmas would travel to the country side of Rockdale, Texas—a town 18 miles from Lexington—to pick cotton. This promising town was established from the opening of the railroad line early in 1874. Settlers began entering in the fall of 1873. Becoming the railroad terminal, this new town became the commercial center of Milam County having a trade territory from the Brazos River to Georgetown and from Giddings north toward Waco. Bell, Burleson, Williamson, Corynell, Milam, Lee and other counties made Rockdale their market town and poured their products into it—notably cattle and cotton. It was reported in the 11/8/1875 issue of the "Galveston Weekly News" that "Over two hundred bales of cotton came to market today and it commands extra prices, Rockdale merchants being content to simply exchange the cotton for goods in Galveston. Three thousand bales were shipped from here during October and about 5,000 this season." Who were the cotton pickers? Negroes from those neighboring towns who were direct descendants of African slaves who had migrated from various geographical areas of the country to live in the state of Texas. Champ Green was one such individual. So each summer to supplement his resources he, his children and other neighboring families joined others in this work venture. Income from the two sources enabled Champ to buy shoes and coats for the children and a bolt of material for Isabel to make garments for the girls and the boys.

Now work and struggle did not totally define the activities of the Champ family. They practiced the Christian faith. Isabel and the children attended weekly the New Hope A.M.E. Church in Lexington, Texas. Champ went occasionally for special events, but most Sundays he had a full day of rest.

In addition to church attendance the family often visited Isabel's brother Thomas Joiner and his family, who lived in the country outside of Lexington. Thomas and his wife, Elizabeth, apparently felt the need to populate the countryside of Lexington. Their contribution in this venue was 17 living, breathing children whose names were Zilla, Penny, Tina, Mamie, Ornalia, Mollie, Gladys, Viola, Erick, Thomas, Jim, Helen, Roy, S. L., Ed, Jenny and Coy—10 girls and 7 boys. When Champ's children saw how these children sat in a circle on the floor to eat at mealtime, Bertha vowed and shared that she was never going to have any children. They all laughed at what they deemed to be a ridiculous promise, especially if she planned to get married. That was the order of things in that day in the Negro families in this small community. The Joiner children too reflected the effects of miscegenation. Two thirds of the children were medium to extremely fair complexioned. One-third was as dark complexioned as midnight. Apparently Thomas was also one of the slave master's children. As a family they were not affected by this difference.

CHAPTER 4

The Challenge

As the children delighted and progressed in the one-room, one teacher classroom serving all grade levels, a bone of contention developed between the Green family children and Ms. Lizzie's 10 children who carried her last name. Ms. Lizzie did not have a husband. Her last name and her children's last name turned out to be her maiden name. The "bone of contention" that developed was the rumor voiced by Henry, a child of another family, who said in a provocative manner while playing in a competitive sport with the Green twins Fate and Minor "Your papa is all Ms. Lizzie's children's papa too." Now those were fighting words, and simultaneously Fate and Minor bellowed out, "Liar! Liar!" And the fight began. Witnessing the action, Ollie runs in the building to tell Mrs. Tonsita, the teacher. The melee was stopped, and the principals engaged were sent home with a 3-day suspension. On their return a parent would have to come with them.

As Fate and Minor walked home they began to talk about how Ms. Lizzie's children would come to their house many times and how their mama Isabel, without any sign of objection, provided Lizzie's children portions of food equal to theirs. Angry and frustrated with their suspensions and the reason for them, Fate stopped walking for a moment and said, "We gotta ask papa about this," to which Minor said, "Yeah, c'us it's not true, is it Fate?" Fate just shrugged his shoulders in disgust.

When the boys got home, Isabel discerned that their countenance was not the same. They were not in that "glad to be home, time to play mode." And she asked, "What's the matter boys?" "Are you in trouble?" "Did you do something you had no business doing? In concert they replied, "No Ma'am." "We just gotta ask Papa something." Isabel was suspicious about their inquiry, but pretended calmness saying, "Okay, he's coming in now, you'll have that opportunity." She left the boys and went into the kitchen because she didn't want to hear what she knew about her husband's infidelity.

The twins ran out of the house to meet their father as he stepped down from the wagon. "Papa, papa," with fear in their hearts they called out. Looking at the boys, realizing something was wrong, he asked, "Okay! What happened today that has you so frustrated?" Fate spoke up. "Henry at school today at lunchtime yelled out where everybody could hear: "Your papa is Ms. Lizzie's children's papa too," and laughed. "Is that true papa?" Champ was surprised at this revelation and its source particularly, but the truth was out, and he had to think quickly on what to say to the twins to put their concerns at rest. So, he told them to come sit on the steps and listen to him. And he began to ask them questions: "Do you see me every day?" "Where am I every night?" "What bed do I sleep in every night?" "Who feeds you, and keep you in shoes and clothes and a roof over your head?" The twins lowered their heads and murmured, "But." Champ fired back. "Listen to me, hold your heads up." "I love your mother, she will always be my wife, and you can take that to the bank." "Now get up and go inside. "I know your mama has a great meal for us." "I don't want to hear anymore about this." The boys got up and Champ swatted them on their buttocks as they went into the kitchen.

Now Lizzie, like Isabel, had parents who were slaves. But Lizzie was not a product of miscegenation. She was the embodiment of one from the Wartuse tribe. She was tall with long legs, thin body, keen features and very dark complexion. She could well have been, if born in the time, a 21st century model. And yes, Champ Green fathered all her children. Still, with both families depending on Champ—the bread winner—he was able to sustain both families with his produce selling, picking cotton which included the children from both families who were big enough and his peanut crop on the farm each year. He was also able to raise a few cattle whose sale at any given time boosted his income. Isabel and Lizzie worked only in the homes in the role of homemaker and help meet.

When Champ looked at Isabel, she knew instinctively what happened, but acted as though nothing had. Dinner that evening was rather silent. There was little or no conversation.

While in bed that night, Ada the feisty one and her partner in crime, Mollie, had a plan of reaction to Henry the whistleblower's declaration the day before that fueled this family inquiry. Now Mollie and Ada were the epitome of Mutt and Jeff. Ada was less than 4 feet tall and Mollie was at least 5 feet 7 inches. And so Mollie, without any of her own ideas asked: "What are we going to do Ada?" Ada the aggressor cunningly responded: "Well as soon as school lets out we're going to run as fast as we can to the bridge over the creek that he has to cross over. He's the only one who has to go over the bridge home. We'll hide under the bridge where he can't see us, and when we hear his little galloping trot touch the bridge we'll make a surprise jump on him and beat him up. We'll teach him to keep his big mouth shout about our family." Mollie agreed that this was a good plan. They would teach him a better lesson than he received in school that day. For these two plotters the school day seemed extremely long. They did not share their plot with anybody not even Betty or Bud their older siblings. For certainly Bud would do any thing Ada asked him to do. They purposely sat close to the door of the one-room classroom and school. And as soon as the teacher rang the school bell at the end of the school day, the two plotters became expert sprinters traveling to the creek, hiding under the bridge, waiting patiently for their adversary—Henry. They knew he was going to fool around at school causing his usual chaos—gossiping and telling lies before he left. So, when they heard his familiar whistle, as he was approaching they knew their plan of action was imminent. As soon as they heard Henry's footstep on the bridge, Mollie the tall one reached up and grabbed him and pulled him down under. As soon as this happened, Ada went on a massive destruction act beating him, tearing his clothes and telling him vehemently that he better not tell anymore lies about her papa. When the girls finished their destructive acts, Ada bellowed out, "Now how do you feel Mr. Liar?" "Let me tell you something else: you better not tell anybody who did this to you and why. Look at you. You will be the laughing stock of the whole school if it is known that two poor little girls beat you up. You better figure out something else to tell your mama how you got a bloody nose, a busted lip, a knot on your head and your clothes almost torn to pieces." The girls left the scene feeling good about their conquest.

Henry did not return to school for four days until his visible bruises cleared up, not to have any questions about who beat him up. At home for Isabel's sake, the conversation about the biological father of Lizzie's children became a 'mum' engagement. And so life for the two odd families of Champ Green went on as the children grew, finished school or dropped out. Bud just didn't go to school much and was a predicted dropout. Activities the children delighted in were school extra curriculum events—ball games, hay rides and end-of-the-year programs and graduation exercises. And they enjoyed the travel to Rockdale, Texas to attend church Association gatherings. And, of course, cupid was in full bloom for the girls. Each had a significant boyfriend, but Champ's rule was 'bible.' They had to be home by sundown. And no one broke the rules. He let the girls know that he would send the boys after them and embarrass them.

Bertha, the eldest girl, who vowed she would never have any children, dropped out of school and married a young farmer named Frank Taylor. Frank was a successful farmer and rancher. He had a great deal of land outside Lexington's city limits where he raised cows and pigs, chickens and turkeys. He planted and harvested fruits and vegetables seasonally. Additionally he planted and harvested an abundance of peanuts. All of these products provided sufficient income for the raising of his family. Though Bertha vowed she wouldn't have any children, she and very fertile Frank had 10 children: 4 girls—Elnora, Isabella (called B. Bell), Louisa, and Bertha; 6 boys—Jimmie Lee, Green, Sherman, Pink, Wilbert and T.M. (called Boy). Two of the children—Bertha and Pink—preceded their parents in death.

Now Ada, the feisty one, and brightest one mentally, was the one her teacher Ms. Tonsita Green saw great potential in. She was in her estimation college material. Well her last year in high school Ada had a boyfriend whose name was Ennis. At the church's pastor's anniversary service, Ada had been designated to give the welcome. She had written a beautiful speech. She practiced, even looking at herself in the mirror. Ada was ready. At the church when the Mistress of Ceremony said profoundly, "Miss Ada Green, one of our finest young members from the Champ Green family will give the welcome, Ada!" Ada rose from the chair looking very pretty in the special dress her mother had helped her design and make. She came to the podium smiling, but she looked out in the congregation and low and behold there was Ennis, her boyfriend. She froze. The smile went away; and it appeared she had lock jaw. Thoughts and words ran through her mind, but she just couldn't open her mouth to speak. And so, she exercised the next best thing. She bowed her head cowardly and ran off the pulpit, and didn't stop running, as she heard the congregation clapping as if she had said something, until she got home. Ennis was in fast pursuit. But when she entered her home, she told Fate her little brother, to lock the door and to tell Ennis that she wasn't feeling well. This affected her so much that she broke off the relationship with Ennis. He was very unhappy, and talked with her brothers. But they knew Ada, and knew she wasn't going to change her mind. They advised him to forget about Ada. They knew their sister and how she would not overcome her embarrassment soon.

Ada, despite this devastating episode in her life, made up her mind to be successful. She watched Isabel cook and sew. She was going to be as great a housewife and mother as Isabel. Isabel would often say to her, "Ada, go find something to do beside watching what I'm doing." And Ada would say, "But mama I just want to be like you when I have a family 'cause you're the best mama as I see in all of Lexington, Texas." Both laughed at this nonsensical assumption. Ada also became more studious. Her school activities and excellent grades were such that Mr. Ledbetter, Ada's second teacher, was so impressed with her academic achievements that he wanted to help this young girl financially to pursue higher education, and so, as she was about to graduate he offered her a scholarship to attend college. Mr. Ledbetter knew the size of the two Green families. With no children of his own, he developed a fatherly affinity to Ada as he watched her growth and development. Well, Ada didn't jump and dance across the room, she stood looking very mature and said, "Mr. Ledbetter I appreciate your kindness. I thank you so much, but I have to tell my parents about your offer and I'll let you know." Her teacher and possible benefactor was impressed with her response to his unprecedented offer and said, "Will you let me know tomorrow? You will need to make an application soon to be able to start in September.

Of course she had to share this with Mollie on the way home for the first family member's reaction to the offer. One would have thought Mollie had been cited for the scholarship as she yelled, jumped up and down and hugged Ada. She said after calming down, "Girl, you need to take it. This is your chance to get to the 'big city' and get our of this one-horse town." Ada laughed and said, "Don't say anything to anybody. I have to break this news after supper to mama and papa." Mollie agreed that she wouldn't say anything about it.

Just as supper was ending, Ada decided to make it a family announcement and she tapped her glass as she had seen her father do to get everybody's attention. Everybody looked up at Ada except Mollie who looked down at her plate smiling. Ada started her brief announcement: "Mama! Papa! At school today Mr. Lebetter said he would give me a scholarship to go to college. Ada and Champ shared questioning glances with the same thing on their mind. Champ broke the silence and asked,

"Ada why is he doing this or wants to do this for you?" Isabel broke in, "Honey what does he want from you?" Ada was rather stunned at the questions and said, "Papa, mama Mr. Ledbetter is a very old man. Some people say he's about 78 years old. One day I heard Mrs. Tonsita tell a parent that he doesn't have a wife and he has no children, and she and her pastor and other church people call him a philanthropist. I looked up that word and it means one who acts to promote human welfare and provides money to those who need it. He selects to give scholarships to one or two students he believes has ability to succeed in college." There was silence. Mollie broke it clapping her hands and stating loudly, "I think she should take it." Fate and Minor joined in the clapping.

Isabel stopping the noise asked? "When do you have to let him know Ada? "Tomorrow mama 'cause I have to get an application, fill it out, and summit it, and receive an acceptance to whatever college I want to attend right away. If I don't accept his scholarship, it will allow him to give it to another student. And Isabel said, "Honey don't forget to pray and seek God's help in making your decision." Ada's prayer that night was the longest she had ever made, and most of the night she analyzed the present status of her family. She had discerned the decline in her father's physical ability to do many of the physical work activities he was accustomed doing. The girls were leaving seemingly at rapid departure. Della and Lena had married and moved to San Angelo, Texas a great distance from Lexington. Cissie was engaged and moving to Temple, Texas where her fiance lived was imminent. Mollie was courting a young private in the army from Cameron, Texas. Ada knew those nuptials would be soon. And she knew Ollie would follow Cissie to Temple, Texas.

As Ada thought about her home situation, she realized that both her father's and eldest brother's lives were rapidly coming to the end on this side of Jordan as her Christian thoughts prevailed. Her mother would be alone and with four younger children (Fate, Minor, Onie and Fannie). She felt her mother needed her during these crucial years, and decided before dawn to thank Mr. Ledbetter for his kindness, but that she would not be able to go to school this year because of her family situation. When she arrived at school that morning, she immediately found Mr. Ledbetter and expressed her appreciation and her decision to remain at home the next year because of her family situation. Mr. Ledbetter was very disappointed, but had great respect for the young woman's mature decision concerning her responsibility toward family needs as she had concluded would be the circumstances of family life of the ensuing year. And as she had surmised about the departure of her sisters, it did happen just as she predicted.

Ada did finish high school, but she became obsessed with feeling that she needed to take over her mother's household responsibilities. She felt she needed to relieve her mother of as much work as she could. She couldn't stand the idea of loosing her mother because she became sick from working too hard. She remembered how sick Isabel was when the twins were born and there was no mid-wife to help her. So she took over the family laundry chores. Using a rub board and tub she washed the family clothes. She had Fannie and Onie the two youngest siblings to assist her in hanging things on the line, and she taught them how to draw the well water she needed for the laundry washing and rinsing. She paid special attention to everything Isabel did in the kitchen because she wanted to be the excellent cook Isabel was. Isabel had the ability to prepare unparalleled excellent tasty meals. She was lauded by neighbors and church members who had the occasion to sample her culinary prowess. She had a unique preparation of squirrel, rabbit, raccoon surrounded with sweet potatoes, venison sausage, roast and back strap. There was no one in the Negro community that could fry chicken like Isabel. Ada became the epitome of her mother in food preparation especially rolls and light bread, pound cake and fruitcake.

CHAPTER 5

The Rockdale, Texas Connection

Just 18 miles away in another small town called Rockdale, Texas established in 1874 was felt to be by its dwellers a town with a great promise and appearance of imminent greatness. It became the commercial center of Milam County because of the opening of the railroad line. A town survey recorded in a July 15, 1874 deed filed showed the town containing 35 blocks of lots. Land on both sides of the track was marked off as a reservation belonging solely to the railroad. The railroad had connections, south, east and west. Starting out in 1880 with a population of 1,185 thus thought to be a promising progressive town had an up and down population trend. For example, in 1920 the population was 3,323 but in 1930 it was 2,204.

Now the Negro population lived on the eastside of the tracks. One such family was the John and Ellen Woods Family. In the eyes of neighbors, the family was affluent. John had amassed a great deal of land and property within and outside the city. It is believed that the family came from Oklahoma.

John and Ellen had three sons—John Jr., Jesse, and Isaac (Ike), and one daughter—Agnes Ellen. None had the progressiveness of their father.

As children they attended the Rockdale segregated public school. Not one completed. John Willie moved to San Antonio, Texas after dropping out, married Rosie Lee Irving, and they had a son they named John. John Willie was endowed with a music talent. He learned to play the piano with excellent skill without ever having a music lesson. But he never did anything professionally with this special talent. Jesse became a nomadic 'jack-leg' preacher traveling by freight train from Rockdale to San Antonio where he sired a son. The child's mother named him Joe Lewis using her maiden name for his last name. Jesse never married her nor did he ever support the child. Agnes Ellen moved to San Antonio and was employed as a cook for a wealthy white family. Her only child born out of wedlock was named Dorothy. Agnes Ellen, however, was successfully married to a gentle gentleman who was called "Mr. Daddy" by all who knew him for reasons unknown. Ellen and her husband had a very nice, impressive large house on Ferguson Street a couple blocks away from the genesis of Artemesia Bowden's establishment of a Negro college in the community. It happened because of the unrelenting work of this exceptional citizen. The school was named St. Phillips College.

Ellen's neighbors were considered upper class. A public school teacher lived next door. Across the street were a doctor's and police officer's families. A Pullman porter and his family lived down the block and a headwaiter in one of the grand hotels down town lived around the corner.

Ike, the youngest, and apple of his mother's eyes completed the 4th grade and stayed in Rockdale to be with and help his mother manage their property in and out of the town following the death of his father—John Woods.

Ellen swiftly had Ike's name placed on the deeds of all the property her husband had acquired because she had more faith in her youngest son than her two older sons primarily because of their desertion from the home place. Concerning her only daughter Agnes Ellen in San Antonio, she felt that she was well established. The matriarch Ellen in Rockdale owned a very nice home with a well-built outhouse a stone throw from her home. She told Ike when he got married, it was his. Ike smiled and gave his mother a 'bear' hug, but had an inward private chuckle because at this season of his life he didn't even have a girlfriend. In fact, he was thinking seriously about joining the army. He had not shared this thinking with his mother. He really did not know how he could break the news to her. Then he thought about the house. Old man Barney had been living in the house since before his father died. And so he resolved in his mind that Mr. Barney could remain in the house until he completed his tour of duty in the army. He just wasn't thinking that he could be sent on the battlefield, be killed, and never come back.

CHAPTER 6

The Social Climate

Church activities in the Negro community of this small town were paramount to the spiritual and social life of the residents. Church Associations had great attendance. They provided a regional community participation as other small towns particularly Lexington, Cameron, Lincoln, Ballenger, Taylor and Giddings church members would travel to Rockdale to participate in the weekend events as the New Hope Baptist Church served as host church. Church services were held with the various preachers from the neighboring towns providing sermons each day during the week of the Association. Combined gospel choirs provided music for the services and gospel concerts. There was a real sense of kononia in all of the attended activities.

Ladies demonstrated their culinary skills in fried chicken and pound cake competition. Young adult Ike sold a special red sweet drink he called "Goliath's blood." And he would yell out, "Come and get your Goliath's blood" to attract potential customers.

When Mr. Barney told Ellen that Ike was planning to go in the service, she cried and prayed privately about it day and night.

CHAPTER 7

The Timely Decision

Ike knew that Mr. Barney, his father's best friend, would be there to help his mother. And so, with some comfort he shared his plan with his mother. Ellen put on a happy face, gave him a bear hug and kiss, holding back the tears, smiled and said, "Take care of yourself son. Don't forget to pray for God's protection and favor wherever you are. And you better write me as often as the sun comes up." Smiling, Ike's careful response was, "I'll try mama" knowing that this was probably impossible. And so this 5 ft 10 handsome, strapping 24 year old named Isaac Hannibal Woods took the popular train, journeyed to Cameron, Texas and was inducted in the U.S. Army April 2, 1918. Having not finished high school, completing only 4th grade his vocation was described as laborer and was assigned to and regarded as an excellent member of the 415 Labor group. Despite his lack of education, he was smart especially in math and he had a special talent similar to his older brother—John. He had an innate music talent. He could play the bugle. And he became the bugler for his unit.

Ike made friends easily with other soldiers in his company, but he had a special affinity for one Private First Class Dan Larkin a couple of years older than he. He was impressed with the fact that he was already married and had a restaurant described as a "Honky Tonk." Young soldiers gathered there to drink beer and get the best fried chicken in town. In fact this was the Negro restaurant preferred by the soldiers. As Negroes they could not eat in the established White restaurants in town.

The first time Ike went to Dan's Honky Tonk Joint and restaurant, Dan introduced him to his wife Mollie. Dan being so proud of his tall mulatto skin colored wife (for Dan's complexion was black as midnight and he was on the heavy side) he said to Ike, "Ike (putting his arms around Mollie) meet my beautiful wife Mollie. I picked her 'cause she was the prettiest of the eight litter of the Champ Green family in Lexington, Texas." Mollie blushed showing her dimpled cheeks and expressive high cheekbones. Mollie, shaking Ike's hand said, "Pleased to meet you Ike. Welcome to our place anytime." "Thank you ma'am." Ike said thinking and laughing to himself. If Dan can get somebody who looks like Mollie surely I can. He also discerned that Mollie despite her tall slender body looked like she could be pregnant. She was, and close to delivery time.

Ike spent a lot of time with the Larkins. Dan talked briefly one evening about Mollie's sister Ada coming soon to help Mollie when the baby comes in a couple of months.

Ada came a week before baby Dorothy was born and was a tremendous help with the baby and the restaurant chores Mollie did. The first weekend Ada was there, many of the soldiers came to the restaurant mainly to see this new girl in town and some interested in seeing Dan's new baby. Well she certainly was Dan's baby. She had her father's skin color, a beautiful little round face, dimpled cheeks and beautiful brown eyes.

Ike was more the curious about Dan's sister-in-law when he came to the restaurant. When she came out of the kitchen to serve a customer a plate, all he could say to himself was "Wow." Dan was definitely wrong in his assessment of the 'prettiest' of the Champ Green litter of girls. There she was petite 5 feet tall, complexion like Mollie's with shoulder length hair. In his estimation, she was just a beautiful package form top to bottom. Not even having a conversation with Ada, he declared to himself,—'this girl is going to be my wife,' and chuckled.

After a few visits to Dan's home and special conversations with Ada, the courtship began, and one moonlit evening as they sat on Dan's and Mollie's porch Ike got on his knees and popped the question. Ada blushing and showing her beautiful pearly white teeth, being aggressive hugged him and said, "Yes." The couple's parents Ellen in Rockdale and Isabel in Lexington approved their engagement.

Now Ike, though young as he was, developed some medical issues such that affected his army career. May 25, 1919 he received an Honorable discharge granted by William Cartinell, Major Infantry U.S.A Commanding at Camp Travis, Texas and was paid in full $92.75 by Gilbert H. Goosey, Major Q.M. Corps including a bonus of $60.00 per Act of Congress approved February 24, 1919.

When Ada returned home after her stay with Mollie and Dan, she and Isabel talked many evenings after the younger ones had gone to sleep about the expectations of a good Christian wife. She had certainly been one despite her husband's infidelity. Knowing she was leaving her mother's home soon, Ada felt the need to instruct her younger siblings about helping Isabel. Fannie, the baby girl, said to Ada, "I know how to do all the things you do because I watched you. And I can do them. I know how to keep Fate, Minor and Onie in line just like you did. Ada had to laugh at the last statement she made, inasmuch as Fannie was a girl and the youngest of the brood living at home.

As Ada began preparing herself for the life changing of marriage, she received a letter from Ike. It wasn't just a love letter but one citing an absolute career change for him. Expressing his continued and unchanging love for her, he wrote that he was being discharged from the army. He assured her that he received an honorable discharge.

This just didn't matter to Ada at all. He was going to still be her husband, and she didn't care about the circumstances of his discharge and what he planned to do for a living. Their wedding plans were still on.

Now Ada realized that Isabel did not have the resources to give her a big wedding, so Ada took the lead and told her mother that she didn't want a big wedding. She told Isabel that she and Ike were going to go to Ballenger, Texas—a small town in Runnels County. In fact this was the town her family had migrated from. She only wanted the necessary people there for the ceremony.

Isabel learning of Ada's plan said to her, "Honey I understand why you're doing this and I love you for understanding, but I'm going to have a dinner for you after the wedding. I'm going to invite our neighbors, your friends and any of Ike's friends he would like to be here. Ada hugging her mother affectionately said, "Thank you mama. I will help you and Mollie will be here to help. And, of course, you have little grown up Fannie who will be a great help or hindrance." And they both chuckled at this factual statement.

And so it came to pass after six months of serious courtship either by visitation or letter, November 22, 1919 Ike and Ada appeared before a judge in Ballenger, Texas to consummate this planned great event. Ada was dressed in a beautiful long white, long sleeved satin dress whose design she had copied from a magazine and made with the help of Isabel, and she wore the appropriate head dress. Ike was dressed appropriately in his military attire not wanting to spend unnecessarily on a store bought black suit he may or may not wear again.

Not only were the necessary people there but Ada's sisters Cissie and Ollie came from Temple, Texas, Bertha and her husband Frank from Lee County and of course little sister Fannie, the twins Fate and Minor and Onie from home. Ike's mother and old man Barney Fannin, his brother John Willie and Sister Ellen from San Antonio, his Jack-Leg preacher brother Jessie and a host of first cousins of the 19 children in the Joiner family came. Mollie was Ada's maid of honor and Dan, Mollie's husband, was Ike's best man. And when the judge said, "I pronounce you man and wife" the great and lingering embrace and kiss took place after which the celebration began.

Isabel feared that she had not prepared enough food for all the people that had just come to witness the ceremony. But, unknowing to Ada, her great friend and neighbor Mrs. Taylor had organized a neighborhood committee to prepare food for this blessed event because she knew of Isabel's financial state. So, when the wedding party reached Isbel's house and she recognized Mrs. Taylor standing at the door, she knew something big had occurred. It had. Isbel's kitchen was laden with specially fried chicken, country ham, collard greens, black eyed peas, sweet potatoes, cornbread, biscuits, pound cake and sweet potato pie. Ada just grabbed her mother's friend, hugged her and whispered in her ear, "Thank you. I know you did this." At the end of the great feast and well wishes to the bride and groom, Ada thanked and acknowledged all the neighbors by name that had made all the particular food items prepared. She stated that their efforts and contributions were truly a testimony of God's goodness and his supplying our needs as was the feeding of the five thousand by Jesus. Isabel not only had enough for everybody there, but she had plenty leftovers for her and the children at home.

At the end of the day, just before sunset, and when most of the 'well wishes' had left, Ike whispered to Ada, "We need to leave before it gets dark. 'Ole' Nellie (speaking of the horse pulling the wagon they were going to travel in to get to the International and Great Northern Train Station) doesn't do to well in the dark and neither do I." They both giggled about this, but Ada directed him to the bedroom where all her belongings had been packed in a large trunk. Ike solicited the help of Fate and Minor to help him put it on the wagon. They rode to the train station so they could drive the horse and wagon back home. Ellen and Ike's brothers returned to Rockdale in the great vehicle called the Model T Ford that John, Ellen's husband, had been privileged to purchase before his death.

On the train Ike talked about his regret that they were unable to have a real honeymoon, and how she felt about old man Barney living in the house with them. Looking at Ike affectionately, Ada said, "We'll have our honeymoon in our bedroom." She had no idea what this marriage consummation physically would mean, although there had been brief conversations with Mollie about what to expect. At 24 years old, Ada was still a virgin. She continued to say, "Old man Barney seems to be a nice old man. It wouldn't bother me at all for him to be with us. In fact I kindah think of him as a father substitute." Ike laughed and hugged his bride.

As the train pulled into the Rockdale station, looking out the window, Ike could see his dad's Model T parked. His brother John had driven in record time to take the family to Ellen's home and to drive to the train station to pick them up and take them to Ike's house. The house was a big house of many rooms his father had acquired in his many real estate transactions. Ellen promised Ike the house when he married. Of course there was the welcome boarder Barney who occupied a portion of the dwelling in the rear of the house—a distance from the nuptial area. The kitchen and dinning areas were shared. A well-constructed outhouse was located a short distance from the back of the house, and there was a huge veranda across the entire front of the house. The house was a model resident east of the tracts in the Negro residential area of the town.

Just before daylight following a night of incomparable bliss by Ada, it was daybreak—a time to start a new day. Smiling and looking at her handsome husband sleeping, she reveled at what had taken place during the night and kissed him lightly on the cheek so she wouldn't wake him up. Reality hit her and she knew it was time for her to get up and do what she had seen Isabel, her mother, do every day. She started out by using the kettle of water on the pot-belly stove and enough cold water to be poured in the wash tub in the special private room for bathing purposes. Ike and Barney were still sleeping as she finished her bath and proceeded to the kitchen to prepare breakfast.

There were fresh eggs in a basket atop the icebox, and she found salt pork bacon and butter in the icebox. She found flour and all the ingredients she needed to make biscuits as she had seen Isabel make. While the biscuits were cooking, she sliced up enough salt pork bacon for the three of them, boiled the bacon for awhile, drained the pan and fried the bacon. She made grits, scrambled eggs and a very strong pot of coffee. The aroma was too much for the two sleeping giants as they woke up and realized something was going on in the kitchen. Ike and Barney bumped into each other trying to get into the wash room to clean up for what they believed to be a great morning breakfast.

Sitting at the table eating, Ike couldn't help but beam with pride at the competent and unbelievable culinary expertise of his young bride. And for more than twenty-five minutes Ike and Barney pinned verbal flowers on this tiny little woman who stood in the kitchen as well as in the bedroom as only Ike knew. Now neither the bride nor the groom had experience in the bedroom, but had gained some instructions from their married siblings. Their siblings' instructions were followed without a hitch. And so Ike and Ada's romance was contagious.

CHAPTER 8

Community Acceptance

Not only did Ada please her husband in every way, but Ellen her mother-in-law was overwhelmed by her personality, her talents and how she believed that she truly loved her son as she observed her persona with him, and how she had made the house the couple occupied a home. Not only could Ada cook but she could sew and make essential items for the house and her own clothing. Ellen wanted to showcase her new and petite daughter-in-law to her friends and neighbors. So, as soon as she felt the in-house honeymoon was over, Ellen went to Ike's house and summoned Ada. She was truly curious about what was about to happen. Had she done anything wrong? She thought. What was Ellen's strange call at the porch? The only thing she could think to say was "What's the matter mother Woods?" Ellen, smiling, replied, "Not a thing. I just want you to take a walk with me."

It was a nice evening for walking. There was sunshine and a cool breeze. Ellen took Ada by the hand and they walked through the neighborhood with Ellen introducing her to the Ledbetters, the Wratts—Mrs. W.B. Wratt being the church clerk, the Goins, The Maze—Ernestine Maze being the church pianist, the Onwines and the Aycocks. They passed by New Hope Baptist Church and Ellen mentioned that this is the church she and Ike were members of. And, in an invitational manner said, "If you and Ike come to church next Sunday, you'll meet more of our neighbors." Ada looking up at her mother-in-law with a big smile said, "Yes ma'am we'll be there Sunday." As they approached Ada's porch, Ada turned in front of Ellen, hugged her, thanked her and asked her to come in and have supper with them. Ellen accepted graciously because deep down she wanted to see if Ada was as good a cook as Ike and Barney had bragged about.

As they entered the house they heard Ike and Barney in the kitchen talking about the war, and they stopped for a minute to listen. Ike was telling Barney about how the war was declared in Serbia July 28, 1914. He continued stating that it was because Archduke (Prince) Franz Ferdinand, the nephew of the Austrian emperor and his wife were killed by a young Serbian as he was driving through the streets of Sarajevo which is a town near the border of Serbia. The Austrians were furious and because the Serbians did not meet their required conditions they would declare war. They did. Ike went on to talk about the other nations who joined in this four year war called World War I—Russia mobilized, Germany declared war on Russia and . . . A firm small voice at the inside kitchen door said, "Okay gentlemen, enough about the wars. You know the United States didn't really get into the battle until 1918 and If my memory is right I believe November 11, 1918 all these fighting mighty countries signed an armistice which was an agreement to stop fighting in a railroad car. So can we talk about more pleasant things while we have our supper especially with mother Woods joining us." The men were speechless and at awe at this young unpredictable young woman who was there in their space being knowledgeable about current events. Finally Ike blasted out, "Sure honey, mama come on and sit over here" as he pulled out the chair. But Ike had to have the last word about the war because he was a soldier. And he said as Ada started setting up the table and placing the food on the table, "Honey I just have one more thing to say, if you don't mind." And he knew she wouldn't mind. So, he proceeded saying, "This was the first time warships and airplanes fought in the air bombing soldiers and civilians." Barney cut him off asking how he knew all this. But before Ike could answer, Ellen said, "Enough, enough about this war. Thank God son you did not have to go and fight and you were blessed to receive a timely and honorable discharge. You know you were in my prayers and this community's prayers." And Barney blurted out, "Amen sister Ellen." Their eyes then focused on Ada as they watched her meticulously place the baked chicken, smothered rabbit, collard greens, baked sweet potatoes and cornbread on the table. And she had a pitcher of fresh lemonade on the side. It was truly a feast for all the partakers especially Ellen. And, so much so that, leftovers were just a few crumbs for the men's hound dogs.

As Ada cleaned the kitchen, Barney took a nap in his favorite chair. Ike walked his mother home, and Ellen talked all the way home telling Ike he'd better treat this girl right with Ike replying comically, "Yes ma'am mamma. I'm going to do just that." And they both laughed out loud. But Ellen, entering her house, knew that her son had found a 'diamond' in the rough.

After four months of absolute bliss by the young couple and the complete acceptance of their tenant, Ike realized two things: 1) His money was getting short despite the peanut harvest and sales and his mother's cash wedding gifts, and 2) Ada was pregnant. Both Ada and Ike were extremely happy, and Ike caused even his neighbors to be excited about this coming event. After talking with Ada briefly about their financial status, Ike decided to set up a Shoeshine business near a busy intersection down town. It was not unusual to see a Negro shining the shoes of White businessmen on the street or in a barbershop or the hotel lobby. Ada had no objection to Ike's decision.

Ada had her own problems. Morning sickness as a result of the pregnancy caused her to exhibit some irritability at times. This temporary side of Ada presented it's being one morning as she was sweeping the veranda when she heard someone calling. "A'nty." When she turned around to see who was talking, this very old White man driving a horse and buggy said "An'ty can you tell me where the Wratts live. Now the 'four year old Ada rose' and vociferously she fired back, "Well I sure didn't know I was your mother's sister." She paused as if to get some kind of rebuttal from him looking directly at him. The old man was too surprised to say anything. And so Ada said, "They live at the end of the block on the corner facing the east." Still startled at this petite young Negro woman's remarks, the old man tapped the horse and traveled on down the road but still turning his head around to see what the young Negro pregnant woman was doing.

Now Barney heard this exchange of words by Ada and the old man, and he truly felt the possibility of some retaliation by the old man or his younger family members. So he staid inside to eliminate what he felt might be confrontational and a danger to Ada in her delicate condition.

At supper that evening, Barney struggled with knowing the gravity of the situation how he could in some way tell Ike what happened. As they were almost finished Barney, in a joking manner to soften the question, said, "Ada why don't you tell Ike what happened this morning with the old dud in the wagon?" Ada had no inhibition about relating the incident and laughing about it. Ike almost choked, but resolved to say nothing that would embarrass Ada in front of Barney, but he definitely had to address the matter in the bedroom where they would be alone. So, jokingly he said, "I bet you surprised him." After which Ada replied, "I sure did." And they all laughed.

Lying next to each other in bed that night, Ike took Ada in his arms and began giving some historical facts about the citizenship of Negroes post slavery treatment. "Honey You've read and heard about the raping and lynching of our people. Well, that's not completely behind us. Some consider us second class citizens not worthy of the same treatment afforded Whites in the country." "Think about it, can we eat in any restaurant we want?" "Can out children go to any school?" "Can we live in any part of town we want?" "Shucks, we even have separate water fountains and no public toilets to use." "Even though we don't have a slave master, our standing in any small southern town is not much higher than the dogs and cats the White man loves and treats better than the dark skinned human beings." "Someday, I believe, things will change and we will have equal opportunity." "But now be careful what you say when you happen to be around a White man or woman." "And believe me, White women can be as cruel as the men." "So, please for my sake and the baby's be careful what you say and how you say it." Snuggling close to Ike, Ada said, "My love, I understand what you're saying, but when I read the Bible—God's word—I find it difficult that some people feel that they are the superior people when God created man and woman and we were all created in his image. But, I will honor your advice and guard by tongue when it is necessary for me to talk to any of the White people here in this town." She kissed Ike on the cheek, turned over and fell asleep.

Ike didn't do much sleeping that night because he really wanted to share with Ada his plan for adding to his income. Now Ike with only a fourth grade education could figure numbers in his head faster than most in his family and circle of friends could with paper and pencil. With a baby coming he realized his income needed to be increased. So, at daybreak, he felt Ada squirming a little, and he thought this was a good time to share his plan. Touching Ada he said, "Honey, I've been thinking with the baby coming and shining shoes is not bringing in much right now, I've decided to go with the next wagon of folks and pick cotton. I understand pay is pretty good right now. I hear a lot of good things about this cotton business from my customers. When I heard one of them say that Texas was the second largest cotton-growing state, I figured I could have needed income from the effort." "Whatcha think?" Cautiously Ada asked, "Which is the largest cotton growing state?" "Maybe we should go there." Ike laughed out loud and said, "Well since you really need to know it's California, but we don't need to go there. There is enough cotton around here to be picked." Ada turned over smiling, looking in his eyes and said, "I'm going with you for more reasons than the money" and laughed. Of course Ike felt because of her condition it wasn't a good idea, but Ada insisted and they were participants for the peak cotton-picking period and Ada was good at it. But during the last two weeks of the cotton—picking season, Ada began having pains. Ike knew they needed to stay home close to Dr. Allens office. Suffering the intermittent pains for three days and the fourth day severe pains began occurring. Ike went and picked up Dr. Allen because he knew Ada was suffering unbearable pains. When Dr. Allen examined Ada and gave her a pill causing her to drop off in a temporary sleep, he took Ike out in the hallway and said to him, "Son you're going to have to make a decision. I can't save them both. You have to choose your baby or your wife." This is the first time Ike cried since he was a child. Ike finally said, "Doc, I want them both, but I know my wife, I love her, I have held her in my arms during this painful period. I don't know the baby. I haven't held him or her in my arms. I know Ada will be devastated by my decision but Doc, save my wife." And it was done.

Now Ike feared how Ada would react emotionally and the physical and mental effect she would experience when she woke up to find out their baby boy was dead. Ike went to his mother, and she, too, was distraught. But she took him by the hand, had him join her on her knees and she prayed. Ike cried.

Soon after Ike returned home, Ada woke up looking and searching for the baby she had birthed. Ike seeing her search and distress said, "Honey, I have something to tell you." He was truly unprepared on how to tell Ada what had happened. Ada knew something was wrong, and it wasn't just the after child birth pain she was experiencing. Out of her mouth came, Where's the baby?" "Where's my baby?" Ike kneeling beside the bed, caressing Ada's face, kissing her forehead, choosing carefully his words said, "You had a beautiful baby boy." And before she could ask the 'where is he' question he said, "Doc tried so hard to save him, but he just couldn't." As he began to tear up he said, "I guess God just has a special plan in His kingdom and took him to be with Him." In the darkness outside, Ada's screams were carried and heard by several neighborhood friends. And so, close neighbors knew something drastic had happened in the Woods home.

CHAPTER 9

Celebration of a Brief Life

The Memorial Services for the tiny baby whose name would have been Isaac Woods Jr. was held at the New Hope Baptist Church was somber with everyone in attendance in tears because they knew how much this young couple wanted a child. The preacher's message was brief but meaningful coupled with advice for all in attendance and ending with a rendering of a portion of Psalm 100 that says "It is he that has made us and not we ourselve. We are His people and the sheep of His pasture." Adding, he said, "Remember our God has a plan for each of us. We have to consider this happening has purpose. To God be the glory."

These words would linger in Ada's mind many weeks with the question, what was this God's plan for her silent baby and her?

Although Ada did her wifely duties, she appeared catatonic to Ike and Barney. They did everything they could to satisfy her—to help her. After more than a month of this remorse, Ada snapped out of it. It was as if God had given her peace of mind. She had been in constant prayer day and night as Ike had observed. He felt her break from her catatonic state was by the grace of God as He dispatched the work of angels through the neighborhood—the Ledbetter, Maze, and Wrath women.

CHAPTER 10

Solving The Financial Situation

As the cotton-picking season ended, Ike knew he had to increase his shoe shining activity.

Now Ellen had cattle in the countryside that Barney took care of after Ellen's husband's death. She also had given Ike several of the animals. Ada had her vegetable garden in the back of their house, and she had a rooster and a bunch of hens in her self-made chicken coup that Barney had helped her build. As Ike talked to his clients while shinning their shoes about his exceptional wife, her garden and her hen's production of fresh eggs every day, his clients began to order dozens of fresh eggs and such vegetables as her corn and okra.

CHAPTER 11

The Unexpected

Just as things appeared to be normal in their three years of marriage, Ike took sick. He was unable to urinate. Barney took him to the hospital in Cameron, Texas in the Model-T. He stayed through the admission process and Ike's bed assignment. But Ike demanded that he leave and go home so that he could tell Ada he was okay.

When Barney returned to Rockdale, he told Ada exactly what Ike had said to tell her. But Ada was uncertain of the facts presented by Barney. She knew what she had to do. She needed to learn how to drive this contraption called the famous Model-T Ford. So she bargained with Barney to teach her how to drive the 'contraption' as she called it. Barney knew that "no" was not an option for this little petite headstrong woman. In a few hours of the day, he taught her.

After the third day of her training, Ada at the break of dawn got up, dressed, put a few garments in a sack and told Barney she was going to Cameron to see about Ike. Thinking she would change her mind, Barney blurted out, "But Ada you have to get gas." And she answered with, "I can do that."

Getting to the filling station, she realized she had to drive through two concrete pillows that stood parallel to each other with barely enough room, as she visualized, to get through to park to put gas in the vehicle's tank. Bravely she gets out of the car, finds an attendant and asked him to drive the car through so she could get the gas she needed. He laughed out loud and said "Lady if you drove the car here, you can drive through this drive through." Praying a little, Ada took the dare. She drove in, got the gas, drove out, and began her travel to Cameron, Texas. She made it to

Cameron and the hospital without a hitch, and completely shocked Ike. But he had a renewed spirit when he saw her.

Ada went to her sister Mollie's house and staid three days after which Ike was released from the hospital in a favorable condition. Ike was truly amazed at this little less that five feet tall woman he married as she cranked up the car, not allowing him to drive, and drove back to Rockdale without, again, a hitch in the execution of the vehicle.

Things resumed in the daily working activities of the couple. Leisure time was also experienced by both. Ike and his buddies—Ralph Maze, Willie Goings, Jake Ledbetter—were skilled hunters who often went to the countryside to hunt and kill rabbits, squirrels and raccoon, and fowl of the quail and dove species. It wasn't just a sport for them. The spoils of their shooting skills provided meat for their families' consumption. Ada became involved with the woman's circle of the church where, in addition to Bible Study, cooking and sewing classes were conducted especially for the young adults of the Negro community. With her skills in these two venues, Ada was an asset. Now the neighborhood women had discussed among themselves how this young woman looked at all times, but they were truly curious about how her hair looked. They all used Madam C. J. Walker's straightening combs to straighten their hair to facilitate ease of combing. So, the straighter the hair the better able they were to comb and style their tresses. But the curious group commissioned Ernestine Maze, the church pianist, to fine out. They all knew Ernestine had a special affinity for this young bride. Walking home after one of the meetings Ernestine, walking beside Ada blurted out, "Ada, honey, I and most of our friends want to know how you keep your hair looking like it does. Just look at mine, and you'll understand." They both had a hearty laugh at Ernestine's revelation. But Ada said, "Sister Maze, I don't see anything wrong with your hair. But you asked me at the right time because this evening I had planned to prepare the two oils I use." As they reached Ada's house she said, "Come on in the kitchen and I'll show you what I mix together." Ada's recipe for the growing oil was:

White Vaseline

4 drops oil of Cinnamon
1 teaspoon oil of Burgamont
1 teaspoon olive oil

Few drops Quinine
½ teaspoon sulfur

White Wax

And recipe for the Pressing Oil (used with the straightening comb):
Same ingredients as the Growing Oil except leaving out the sulfur and white wax.

Ernestine marveled at this young woman's skills. She went home with the assurance that if she prepared these two oils and used them her hair would look like Ada's. What Ernestine didn't understand was that Ada's hair, because of her heritage, was not as kinky as her hair. But, Ernestine believed when she prepared and used the oil her hair looked like Ada's. It didn't.

CHAPTER 12

A New Blessing

Almost a year following their baby's death, Ike received a letter from a cousin in Oklahoma. Mary Ann wrote that she would be in Rockdale soon and she had a favor to ask them. Within a week of this correspondence for Ike, Ada received a letter from her sister Ollie in Temple, Texas informing her that August 5, 1919 she had become the mother of a little girl she named Laura Bell. Now Ada knew Ollie wasn't married and she wondered who the child's father was. Responding to Ada's letter in which she asked Ollie who the baby's father was, in a brief letter because she felt obligated to do because of her secret plan, she gave the name of Sam Maxwell. Ada didn't know Sam, but she was grateful that Ollie could give a name because she knew her sister did not always exercise Christian values in her behavior. Ada wrote Ollie a congratulatory letter and a "hope to see you and the baby soon" ending.

Mary Ann arrived by train a couple of days later. Ike went to the train station to pick her up. To his surprise, she held by hand a tiny toddler. But Ike acted as though he knew she had a child. Greetings and very little conversation were exchanged between them on the way to Ike's house. Ada was standing at the door waiting anxiously to meet this cousin from Oklahoma. As the three approached the steps and veranda, Ada was overwhelmed as she saw the beauty of the tiny toddler who held her mother's hand so tightly. She was the most beautiful child Ada had seen. She had big brown eyes, caramel color complexion and long—very long locks of light brown hair. Ada knew right away that she was biracial. Ada opened the door with a hearty welcome, picking up the child as they entered caressing her and kissing her on he check. The little girl seemed okay with this stranger's special attention to her as she put her arm around Ada's neck as they walked inside. "And your name is?" Ada asked. Quietly the child said, "Carrie Ann." As they sat in the living room, Mary Ann talked briefly about the train ride, but nothing definitive was stated by Mary Ann concerning the purpose of her visit. Ada broke the ice by saying, "I know you both are hungry and I have dinner already prepared."

As they sat around the dining room table, Barney walked in, and introductions were made. He, too, was struck by the child's beauty. Conversation during the meal was small talk as Mary Ann evoked chuckles from the family as she talked about the segregated coaches, and how the Pullman Porter, the Conductor and the passengers looked at her and Carrie Ann in the Negro coach.

After dinner, Barney's retiring to his room, Carrie Ann falling asleep and put to bed, Mary Ann began telling her story and why she had come to them. She confided that she was a single parent with no support from the child's father who could not even claim to be the child's father. She ventured to say she knew about the loss of their son at childbirth, and how they might consider her proposal. She was giving up her child for adoption, because she had no means financially to care for her. And she wanted her child to grow with two loving parents, and she believed they would be willing to accept that role. Ike was startled, but he could see the gleam in Ada's eyes, concerning this offer. Ike looked at Mary Ann and said, "Mary Ann, Ada and I will have to sleep on this, and we'll let you know in the morning. Well, Ada didn't sleep much. All she could think of was that this beautiful baby girl could be theirs. At 5:30 the next morning, Ike was awaken by Ada's touch. Simply, she said, "Ike, we have to keep her." Half sleep, Ike asked, "You're sure?" "Yes," was Ada's simple but emphatic answer.

After breakfast Ike, Ada, Mary Ann and the child went to attorney Philips' office to do what was necessary to adopt the child. All documents were constructed and signed and recorded. By this legal process the child was now Ike's and Ada's child.

The next morning, on the way to work, Ike took Mary Ann to the train station while Ada took Carrie Ann in the back yard showing her the chickens, how she gathered the eggs, her garden (especially the tomatoes) and the family dog Rover. The child seemed overwhelmed by the things she saw and the questions she asked.

When Ada heard the noise of the car in front of the house she knew Ike had returned, and she feared the reaction of the child. Her fear was realized when the little girl ran to Ike asking, "Where's mama?" "Where did you take her?" Ike picked her up caressing her, not knowing what to say, said, "Oh, she'll be back soon." And as Ike was putting the child down, she looked up at him smiling and said, "I know, she'll be back tomorrow." Ada and Ike exchanging glances surmised that the child had been left with others before.

Life seemed complete for Ada as she treated this little toddler like she was a doll. She made her new clothes, cooked her favorite foods, and as it happened to be the week of the Baptist Convention being held at their church, Ada was involved in doing many things at the convention—especially the food. This was the perfect opportunity to introduce her new baby girl to neighborhood friends especially Ralph and Ernestine Maze. Everyone was happy for Ike and Ada because they knew of their first born birth tragedy.

Now Ike who mixed a red concoction of a drink he called Goliath's Blood for sale to the convention attendees constantly talked about the little girl to his friends. The child running back and forth from Ada to Ike's stand seemed happy with Ada and Ike.

CHAPTER 13

Another Dependent

Nineteen twenty-three Ada received a disturbing letter from her sister Ollie. Ollie lived with Cissie, an older sister, in Temple, Texas. The content of the letter revealed that she had not married, but had a two-year old daughter named Laura Bell born August 5, 1919. She was having financial problems and Cissie and her husband Magnus couldn't continue this burden of the two of them. She wanted to know if Laura Bell could stay with them for a while until she found work and a new place to live. Ada was shocked and concerned that Cissie had not informed them about Ollie's pregnancy.

As she sat on the veranda reading the letter and watching Carrie Ann playing with Rover in the yard, from her peripheral side view, she discerned a figure of a woman approaching. She called to Carrie Ann who came running to her. And as the child saw the figure coming toward the house, she jumped up and down in joy saying, "Here's come my mama. I told you she'd be back." It was Mary Ann. Ada was devastated because she knew in her heart why she had come back. Much conversation transpired as Barney took the child for a walk.

As Ada saw the tears forming in Carrie Ann's eyes despite the legal adoption papers they had on the child, that night in bed she said, "Ike we can't keep her. I know how she feels. I know the hurt she has experienced. We have to give her back." Saddened by this new development, Ike weighing his wife's judgement in the matter conceded that it was the right thing to do. He went to the room Mary Ann and the child were occupying, told her their decision and that he would take her and the child to the train station on his way to work.

Ada cried most of the day, but she knew that God would be pleased with the decision she had made.

Several days went by before Ada gave Ollie's letter to Ike to read. The first thing came out of his mouth was, "Do you want to do this?" Ada, searching for Ike's approval answered, "How can we say no to a child that needs our help because of an undeserving mother?" Ike consented because he had no defense against Ada's logic.

A telegram was sent to Ollie that said, "Yes, bring the child." Two days later, early in the morning, Ada heard the noise of a vehicle in the front of the house. She knew it was Ollie and her child. She nudged Ike to wake him up. Ada hurried to the door with Ike following behind her. The two hugged each other, but Ada picked up the four-year old child and affectionately kissed her on the cheek. She handed her to Ike and he did the same. Laura Bell was not at all the beauty Carrie Ann was. She was small in statue, medium brown skin, brown eyes, kinky short black hair, but pretty little legs and a body one could surmise would develop into model possibility, and she had an insatiable smile and behavior with Ada and Ike. It was as if she knew them all of her brief—life's journey.

As they sat down for dinner including Magnus, Cissie's husband, who brought Ollie and the child in his car from Temple they engaged in small talk about the travel. After dinner, and as soon as Laura Bell fell asleep, Ollie and Magnus left returning to Temple.

The next day as Ada watched Laura Bell playing with the homemade rag doll, Ada knew exactly what she needed to do to her hair. And she envisioned the many little outfits she would make for her. Motherhood and fatherhood were a natural for Ike and Ada the following years. Ada trained the child to be a real asset in performing daily tasks. She helped Ada in the kitchen and the house cleaning. She fed the chickens, gathered the eggs and handed Ada clothes pins to hang the washed clothes on the line. She was a happy child as Ada observed her playing with Rover, the dog, and the Ledbetter children who were neighbors.

CHAPTER 14

Crisis Abound

Now tragedy seemed always to happen in the lives of this young couple. Ada learned her older sister Della in San Angelo, Texas had died January 5,1924. Ada was indeed mournful about her big sister's death, but knew that she would be unable to travel to San Angelo for her funeral. And so she prayed for her family and sent a long inspirational letter to Della's family.

Ada was truly distraught about this loss of her sister in this far east Texas city. Within this same month, another loss occurred in Rockdale, Texas. Ike and Ada mourned the death of Ellen, Ike's mother. Ellen had a great deal of foresight about her children, specifically her sons. She saw the potential of her youngest son, and so in her will she made Ike the beneficiary of all the property her husband had acquired and she had not sold. Not one of Ike's siblings protested his being made sole heir to all the existing property. Perhaps they felt guilty because they had done nothing to help Ellen in the management process after the death of their father. Ike was there for her even in the short time he was in the army.

CHAPTER 15

An Unexpected Change

On a visit to Lexington to see Isabel and give her a first view of her granddaughter Laura Bell, Ada found out her sister Mollie and her husband Dan in Cameron, Texas had separated. She had moved back to Lexington, Texas in a 'shot gun' designed house next door to their home place, and she had a live-in companion who had suffered a stroke and was paralyzed on his left side.

What seemed unbelievable to Ada and Ike was the fact that Mollie and her friend Mason would make weekend travels to Cameron and go to Dan's place for their leisure activity. In addition, Mollie's little girl stayed with her father Dan in Cameron. To Ada and Ike all seemed stranger than fiction, and they often joked about it.

CHAPTER 16

New Beginnings

For the next seven years Ike's and Ada's life experiences, one might say, were rather normal for a Negro couple living in a small town in the segregated south. Ike worked hard overseeing the land he inherited, continuing his shoeshine enterprise on weekends mostly and picking cotton during the summer season. Ada did not work outside the home except during the cotton-picking season. She and Laura Bell went with the cotton pickers. Ada did her share of the picking, and little Laura Bell had a great time riding on the Ike's sack, occasionally trying to pick the cotton as she saw the way Ike and Ada did. In reality, she had more fun running through the rows playing with the neighborhood children.

CHAPTER 17

The Secret

In November 1929 Ada had a secret. She didn't want to share with anyone because of what she had experienced early in her marriage. But it was a secret she knew she couldn't keep because in three months her physical appearance would begin to change. Ada was pregnant. She was so happy, but concerned about what she needed to do to prevent the loss of another child. So Ada's day and night prayers included her petition to God to give her the strength to deliver this child without complications that would cause another infant death. Even though she tried to keep her secret, Ike knew from the beginning, but waited patiently for her announcement. He, too, prayed for God's favor as he noticed Ada praying a little longer than usual.

CHAPTER 18

The Dorothy Factor

Just when the couple felt a normalcy in their lives, another bombshell hit them. Ike's sister Ellen in San Antonio, Texas sent a pleading letter for their help. Her only daughter, Dorothy now eighteen, was in 'family way'—a nice phrase for 'pregnant.' It was pretty customary in those days when this happened, the pregnant girl would be sent to relatives preferably in another town. Ike and Ada were shocked at the knowledge and the request. Ike was really concerned about Ada with the close proximity of the time of the expected births. Dorothy was to deliver in April and Ada in July.

After sleeping over the matter, Ada, with her altruistic spirit woke Ike up and said, "Send your sister a telegram and tell her its okay to bring Dorothy. We'll take care of her." "But Ada," Ike started saying. Swiftly Ada cut him off and said, "Do it Honey. We can manage." Ike grateful for the decision and request Ada made dressed and hurried to Western Union to send the message.

Dorothy traveled by train to Rockdale. The family met her at the station. When she looked at Ada she was surprised to see what a small person she was. The family embraced her, but Dorothy's countenance did not change. She was angry about her circumstances—the fact that she had to leave her home in the big city to come and live with people, though relatives, she did not know in this very small town. Ada recognized immediately that she had to do something to change the spirit of this young woman, and with her innate psychiatric skills, she began by talking to Dorothy as if she were her equal as an adult going through some physical changes that neither was exactly proud about. But talking together on the porch in the cool of the evening while Barney, Ike and little Laura Bell cleaned the kitchen, Dorothy began to develop an affinity for her uncle's petite wife. Not knowing the gender of their unborn babies, they talked and laughed about funny names for either a boy or a girl. The men inside could hear their laughter, and Ike was truly proud of his unbelievable little wife. He didn't mind so much the need of household chores he was doing because he could see the change in his niece's attitude. Dorothy's presence was also beneficial to Ike and Ada. It allowed them to have some individual leisure activities on Saturdays. Ada loved to fish and Ike loved to hunt. So, with a built in babysitter for Laura Bell, Ada and her fishing partner, Ernestine Maze (the church pianist) and W.B. Wratt (the church clerk) went fishing. Ada was good at this fishing endeavor generally bringing home a catch sufficient for family dinner. Ike and his skillful hunting buddies Jack Wratt (husband of W.B.) and Ralph Maze (husband of Ernestine) likewise would have a sufficient kill too—raccoon, rabbit, squirrel or birds for an evening dinner.

CHAPTER 19

A Time of Solace and Transition

the next three months activities of the family were simply work by the provider—Ike and homemaking chores, childcare and self-appointed counseling by the homemaker—Ada.

On the morning of April 9, 1930, Dorothy came into the kitchen where Ada was preparing breakfast and said, "Aunt Ada I don't feel good, I'm having every once in a while severe pain right here," pointing to her abdomen. Ada knew what was going on having had the experience eleven years before. She instructed Dorothy to go lie down informing her that it was time for her to become a mother, and she sent Barney to get Dr. Allen and to take Laura Bell to Ernestine's house to stay until suppertime.

Dorothy's water broke just as Dr. Allen entered the house. As he entered the bedroom looking at Dorothy he figured that this was going to really be a challenge. But, before he could begin the normal routine in delivery of a newborn, Dorothy's baby was making her debut. Allen was shocked that in no way he had to say the usual "push" intermittently to the pregnant young women. With one "push" being declared and one "breathe" and the prospective mother seemingly having very little or no pain in this process. Announcing her independence with a resounding cry eight pound, perfectly normal Agnes Ellen Neal was born. Both mother and baby were in excellent physical condition as attested by Dr. Allen saying to Ada, "Well I know they are going to be find with your nursing skill," laughing as he left the house having been paid for service.

From the very young (Laura Bell) to the senior household member (Barney), all were excited about this very vocal new born. Ada, of course, had some apprehension about Dorothy's behavior, which she observed as a detachment from the usual mother/child connection. In bed that night she convinced Ike that Dorothy and the baby should stay with them for at least six more weeks before returning to San Antonio. Ike was surprised at Ada's suggestion as he thought about her soon to be going through the same childbearing experience as Dorothy, and he remembered what she had experienced with the loss of their first born son. To keep from causing her stress, Ike also recognized the burden he had with three additional mouths to feed and an extra one to clothe. Aside from the funds he inherited, his shoeshine business, and the small amount of rent he received from Barney his income was gradually getting less than his expenses. So, he was extremely eager for the cotton-picking season to begin.

The second week of May Ada helped Dorothy to pack her things to travel. She baked a pound cake and her special fried chicken for the travel. Ike transported Dorothy and the baby to the train station. Ike felt like Dorothy really didn't want to go home, but she knew she had to.

CHAPTER 20

Expectations Fulfilled

As July grew near the fear factor for Ada set in. She insisted that Ike join her in evening prayer in which she prayed that God's grace would be sufficient at the time her baby would be in her arms. Ever so often tears would flow during her prayer as she remembered her birthing ordeal nine years before.

Five o'clock in the morning of July 17, Ada nudged Ike to wake him up saying, "It's time. Go get Dr. Allen." Ike was perplexed and dazed. Could he get Dr. Allen to come to his house this time of the morning? He feared the consequences. His adrenaline hit high levels such that he was dressed and on his way within ten minutes. It would take more than 30 minutes to get the doctor and return. In the mean time Ada suffered her pain in silence so not to wake Laura Bell and Barney. Her contractions were coming faster than expected. Fear was about to creep in when she heard the front door open and Ike and the doctor entered the bedroom. Doctor Allen told Ike to go on the porch and he would come and get him when he could see his baby. Ike was obedient and went and sat on the porch. In less than thirty minutes Dr. Allen went to the porch where Ike was. Ike, getting up with great anticipation heard the Dr. grimly say, "She put me out, Ike. You have to hope for the best. She's having difficulty." Ada suffering constant severe pain and the fear of losing another child, she remembered her mother who had successfully delivered her twin brothers without a doctor or a midwife. So, she prayed, got out of the bed, got on the floor and that Thursday morning at 6:30 Ike and the doctor heard a newborn's cry. Both ran in the bedroom to see Ada back in the bed holding her six-pound baby girl. Ike cried, and the doctor did too. But Dr.

Allen knew he had to do what doctors do during this process and he did. He let Ike know after examining mother and baby that each was fine and in good health. Ike had not had this rush of joy since he was a boy sitting at a fishing hole with his father and catching his first fish. He looked at this tiny baby that he could claim to be his child, and he believed she was looking directly at him with anticipation. Ada had fallen into a deep sleep—most often the usual after childbirth. Now Ike perplexed as to what he was to do if this tiny little creature started crying. So he carefully bundled her up in her blanket, and carried her into the living room and sat down. Barney watching Ike's stress went over to the victrola and put a record on that was a soft spiritual number. In a very few minutes the newest family member was sleep. Now Laura Bell, now eleven years old, was not too thrilled about this newcomer. Already she could feel uncle Ike's affection for her waning as she peeped around the dining room door and observed his 'happy face.' So she tipped into the bedroom where Ada was to determine if she, too, was gloating about this newcomer, but found her sleeping. To get some satisfaction, she went out to the back yard. She sat on the steps, watched the chickens, especially the rooster as he chased the hens, their flight from him and, of course, there was her special friend Rover the dog she could at least hug and feel some affection from.

Inside, Barney watching Ike and the sleeping infant told Ike he could put her in the crib because she was going to be out for a while. As obedient as a small child, Ike got up and did exactly what Barney suggested. And he thought why would that be a plausible statement from Barney since Barney didn't have a wife and he certainly didn't have any children. But, Ike respected his wisdom. After putting the baby in her crib, Ike started out the front door. Looking back, however, at Barney's surprise look he said, "Watch them Barney, I'm going to run down to the corner and tell Ralph and Ernestine—two of Ike's best friends. This couple had been married for a long time but had no children. It appeared that Ernestine was barren.

Hearing the great news from Ike, Ralph put on his shoes and Ernestine put on her hat and blurted out, "Lets go see what we have been praying and watching for." For they had knowledge of Ike's and Ada's first lost.

As Ada was still sleeping, they tiptoed in the bedroom to see the newborn. When Ernestine looked down at the sleeping doll recognizing how small she was, said, "I just have to call her 'Wee Wee'." And so, the child was branded for life with a nickname before she was given her given name.

Returning to the living room, they sat and talked for an hour about this baby's possibilities. Ernestine was going to teach her how to sing among other things, and they all laughed about who and what this baby girl was going to do and be growing up in Rockdale, Texas.

As Ernestine looked up and saw Ada standing at the door, she jumped up, went over, gave Ada a bear hug whispering congratulations to her for her success in bringing 'Wee Wee' in the land of the living. Ada was startled when she heard the name 'Wee Wee' but she didn't react. She would certainly be talking to Ike about it when Ralph and Ernestine left.

Now Ernestine was considered somewhat as the town chronicler as she was the usual neighborhood bearer of good or bad news. By the following evening everybody in this small community knew about Ada's baby girl. The next two days Ike's and Ada's home became a revolving door for the visitation of the Negro families in this small community.

During the following weeks, out-of-town visitors who came to see the blessed gift were Ada's sisters—Mollie and Bertha and little sister Fannie from Lexington and the countryside, Cissie and Ollie from Temple, Texas. Bertha, the oldest was concerned about the name 'Wee Wee' and challenged Ada about it. Ada laughed and told her big sister that was her nickname and that she had been given the name of Dolores Maxine. Bertha was truly relieved. Ada, thinking to herself and chuckling why would Bertha (called Betty) be so concerned when she had named one of her boys 'Pink', another 'Green' and the youngest son 'Boy' with the given legal name of 'T. M'. She and her husband Frank must really have lost it branding their sons that way.

CHAPTER 21

Plot Of A Novice

For the next seven months the Ike Woods household seemed to be in normal family daily living. Ike was picking cotton and keeping his weekend shoeshine business active, Ada at home with the baby and doing wifely chores, Barney taking care of the yard and the outhouse and Laura Bell going with Ike on the cotton-picking ventures. Ike and Ada sensed that she wasn't too happy about the newcomer.

There was a memorable childish act by Laura Bell to compound the couples' thoughts about her. As Ada was doing household chores, Laura Bell asked if she could take the baby in the back yard and hold her until she went to sleep. Ada consented, but was curious about Laura Bell's intent. So, incognito on the inner side of the back screened door she watched Laura Bell stoop over and pick up a sizable rock. She thought she was going to drop the baby and was tempted to rush out and get the baby. Before she did, she saw that Laura Bell was in control. She observed her placing the rock down in front of the hanging swing where she was preparing to sit. When she sat down and started pushing herself back in the swing, Ada knew what her inent was. She was going to drop the baby on the rock to get rid of her. Ada rushed out in time to prevent the drop, took the baby, took Laura bell by the hand and brought her inside. She placed the baby in her crib, put a sugar-tit in her mouth so she wouldn't cry from the strange activity. Her attention was now directed to Laura Bell who was crying and saying, "I'm sorry a'nt Ada. Seeing this hurt child, Ada took her in her arms to calm her. She explained to her that this baby did not change Ike's and her feeling and their love for her. She wanted her to truly understand that. Looking up into her aunt's eyes the child believed her. She dried her eyes, hugged and kissed Ada on the cheek and said, "I just thought you didn't want me no more." Ada hugged her assuring her that was not true. And she took Laura Bell into her bedroom where the baby was, tucked her in her bed and told her to take a nap, and Wee Wee would surely wake her up when she got hungry and started to cry. The eleven-year old rose up, hugged Ada again still tearing up. Ada kissed her and left the room. Laura Bell went into a serious thinking mode. She loved her aunt and uncle. They treated her like she was their own daughter, and she definitely did not want to go to her mother Ollie in Temple. To herself she thought, I can't do a stupid thing like I tried to do with the baby, and she fell asleep. Ada didn't tell Ike about the incident.

CHAPTER 22

A Phenomenal New Gadget

July 1930 through March 1931 family activities of the Woods family seemed rather normal—work, church, fishing and hunting. At Christmas time Ike bought a radio. Everybody in the household was overwhelmed at what they could hear coming from this wooden box. One time Barney heard a song he really liked and he shouted out, "Ada, play that one again." Ike and Ada had a big laugh over that request. Ike, laughing said, "Man we can't do that this is a radio not a Victrola. You see we didn't put a record on it. All we can do on this gadget is turn it off and on and change the station to listen to whatever program we want to hear. On some stations some people are just talking and giving the news." They all laughed including Barney.

CHAPTER 23

Growth, Development, Tragedy

Now feisty little Wee Wee began her walking debut at eight months to everyone's surprise, especially her Godparents Ernestine and Ralph Maze. Ernestine was so fascinated by her that on Sunday mornings she would take her from Ada and set her on the piano stool next to her while she played the piano.

It only took a few months later that Wee Wee talked and could hold a complete conversation. Ironically and surprising while sitting on her fathers lap on the porch as he talked to his hunting buddies, one of them blurted out a renown yarn about a hunting spree. And this tiny creature looked at the unbelievable yarn speaker and blurted out, "That's a yie" startling all the men. But they knew what she meant—he was telling a lie, but she just hadn't mastered the letter "L" sound. They all burst out laughing with a few saying, "You're sure right baby. That was a lie." She giggled, and Ike didn't know what to say because she had not said a word before that. Fast developing her communication skills conquering those letters she had difficulty with, she became the novelty child in this compact Negro community. Ernestine taught her a poem, and this little lady thought every time there was a program at the church she was supposed to speak. Whether she was on program or not she would break away from Ada, go stand in front of Ernestine and very proudly say,

> "Here I stand on two little chips
> Won't you kiss my sweet little lips"

Pointing at her lips, the congregation roared with hand clapping and laughing until the voice of the Mistress of Ceremony began to get their attention as she also clapped. Wee Wee would bow as Ernestine had taught her and go back to Ada and sit down.

In this seemingly normal existing of the Negro populace, many questioned their ability to rise above second class citizenry. Many evenings Ike and Barney sat on the porch talking about matters of a political nature. One evening Ike asked, "Barney do you think there will come a time when this racial divide will change? I mean will there ever come a time that we all can drink from the same water fountain, stay in the same community or hotel, eat in the same restaurants and my little girl can go to the same school Mary Jane across town goes to?"

"Well Ike, I'll put it to you as best I know how. It will happen one day just not in my time or your time. I say that because I believe God and his sovereignty. What he did for the Israelites he'll do for us. But the time for change is set by God's timetable. Oh yes he's going to work through some more brave Negroes and some chosen Whites. Some help could come with the election of the next president of the United States. Because with the present President Herbert Hoover not much or any change has happened. In fact the country is in what the politicians call a depression. Some millionaires have jumped out of windows committing suicide because they lost all their money. Look at us, we don't have much, but we haven't lost anything. I believe what the Bible says—God, our provider, will supply our every need not our wants. Some of those people who lost a lot were greedy and probably did a lot of things that weren't legal to get what they had. But change is coming. It might happen when your little girl goes to college or finishes college. You see how long I'm predicting the kind of change we need is going to happen. God's going to anoint some more strong fighters for our cause like Frederick Douglas, Sojourner Truth and Harriet Tubman. Well I've preached enough Ike, you better get to bed. You got an early rise." Ike responded, "I think you're right about everything you said. I just hope my little girl will experience good change. You're right I do need to get to bed. I Haven't been feeling too good lately, but I don't want Ada to know. But, I'm thinking about going to San Antonio where Ellen and John Willie are. They seem to be doing okay. I sure do believe there are more job opportunities there than here. I know I have a problem just going through the fourth grade, but I'm good at math and I have other skills too. Keep me in your prayers Barney and have a good night's rest. I'll see you at breakfast."

The next morning as the day usually started, Ada was up in the kitchen preparing breakfast for the household. Usually Wee Wee joined her mother within the hour, but Ada noticed that she had not joined her and was not doing her usual walking around the kitchen as if she had some real chores. Also, she would take her rag doll and put her in her homemade doll's chair as if the doll were going to eat also. Carefully checking that there was no danger of the food burning, she went in to check on the toddler. Wee Wee was wide—awake but with a questioning look on her little face. "Are you okay baby?" Ada asked. "I can't move my legs mama," "Let's see. Are you sure? Come on let me stand you up on the floor." The child was right. She could neither stand on her own nor walk. Ada panicked calling Ike who was leaving the outhouse in the back yard. He ran in and witnessed what Ada was panicking about. "I'll go get Dr. Allen and bring him here. He'll know what to do." Breakfast was on hold because no one was exempt from personal feelings about this crisis. This little girl had become the heartbeat of this family with her ability to do things far beyond the expectation of a two and a half-year old.

Returning Ike took the doctor in the bedroom where Ada and the child were. Giving the child a preliminary examination, he had no answer for the cause of her condition or knowledge of how to correct or do anything for the condition. He did mention to Ike privately about the possibility of infantile paralysis (Poliomylitis) as the newly elected president of the United States Franklin Delano Roosevelt suffered and was permanently paralyzed and could not walk. He told Ike that he was going to have to do some research to find out what he and they could do to restore her mobility. Walking the doctor to the front door, Ike asked him how much did he owe him. The doctor shook his head indicating that he didn't charge the family anything, knowing that he had not solved their or the child's problem and really had nothing positive to offer them except hope. Everybody in the household, the god-parents and the closest neighbors took part in providing the services of carrying the child wherever needed. Ike was the primary provider for this service. Ada rubbed her baby's legs with olive oil daily and prayed to God for her recovery. As they continued to attend church services with the child, the church body prayed for God's healing power on the child. Now Barney explained to the young couple that despite all the prayers rendered that were truly necessary that our desire and want for healing which he felt would surely happen and their time for the healing was not necessarily God's time to make it happen. He advised them that they needed to exercise their faith in God. Ada needed to continue her daily application of the oil and rubbing of the legs, and he reasoned with this advice that according to God's word—"Even so faith, if it hath not works is dead being alone." And he went on to quote the rest of the statement by the Apostle James that says, "Yes a man may say thou hath faith, and I have works. Shew me thy faith without thy works, and I will shew thee my faith by my works." He advised Ada to keep up the works and the faith. He told Ike his faith and works of carrying the child wherever she needed to go was indicative of his works and to do it as long as necessary.

Ike's plan for going to San Antonio and the possibility of relocating was definitely placed on hold.

Weeks and month's passed in which the couple's daily activities were first the welfare of the child even taking her back to the doctor in hope but to no avail. Ike continued on his daily shoeshine business and once having a slice of Ada's pound cake with him shared a piece with a 'sweet-tooth' White client that found it so delicious the he wanted to purchase one every Saturday. Thus began Ada's culinary enterprise. Other White clients began to request the same. This income gain was a plus for them during this crisis period of twelve months.

One evening as Ike had put a record on the Victrola, Wee Wee started squirming on Ada's lap. Reluctantly Ada stood her up on the floor, and she began to dance to the music. Every member in the house witnessing this little girl's dancing as a real come back from a year of complete paralysis was at awe. Tears of joy flowed. Ada went into the bedroom for a prayer closet experience, got on her knees and prayed a thanksgiving prayer unparalleled by any pulpit preacher.

From that day on the child was never stricken again by this malady.

CHAPTER 24

A New Beginning

With the baby's miraculous health change, Ike resumed his plan to go to San Antonio and scout for employment in the big city. They did have a slight problem—Laura Bell, Ada's niece who had become seemingly a permanent addition to their family. Ike knew his sister Ellen's temperament as a result of her daughter Dorothy's having a child out of wedlock. Ada and Ike decided to take Laura Bell to Ollie, her mother, in Temple, Texas for a temporary stay until they were able to relocate in San Antonio. On Ada's suggestion, Ike sent a telegram to Ollie briefly telling her their plans. And when they should arrive in Temple. Ada really depended on her sister getting this message. She sat down with Laura Bell and explained in detail their moving plans and that as soon as they had a house of their own, they would send for her. Ada could see the hurt in the twelve year old little girl's eyes. She did not want to go back to Temple for reasons she had not readily shared with Ada. And she was afraid to now as she thought of what the consequences might be if she really shared her true feelings about the matter. So she sat quietly with a foreboding expression on her little face. Ada sensed it, put her arms around her and said, "Don't worry, It won't take long for us to get moved and settled in San Antonio. And remember your aunt Cissie will help your mom. I'll make sure of that when I talk to Cissie. You know she doesn't have any children, and she will be as happy as we have been to have you here with us." Laura Bell got up, looking somewhat relieved of her imminent circumstances said, "A'nt Ada I'm going and look in the hen house and see how many fresh eggs are there. That Rhode Island Red hen lays a lot." Ada smiled and gave her a positive nod.

For their travel the next morning, Ada baked a pound cake and fried a chicken so they would have something to sustain them, inasmuch as they were not privileged to eat in restaurants they passed on their way. And, they did not know of any Negro cafes that were on the road they had to travel.

Ike got up early and had the Model T serviced and filled with gas because he didn't want to encounter any problems on the way.

CHAPTER 25

An Undesirable Reception

When they arrived in Temple, Ada was most apprehensive about how Ollie would react to seeing her child that she had had no bonding relationship with since she left her with them. She was not at Cissie's house when they arrived, but Cissie acted like she was the child's mother reaching out to her embracing her, trying to make her feel that she was wanted and welcomed in her home as she had been in Ada's home. As Cissie's husband Magnus and Ike went outside and talked about hunting and possible job opportunities in the big city, Cissie turned the radio on so Laura Bell might be entertained. Ada placed the baby in Laura Bell's lap as Cissie nudged her to follow her to the bedroom. As they entered the bedroom, Cissie began telling Ada about Ollie's problems and how her behavior became entrenched when she learned she was bringing Laura Bell to her. She assured Ada that she and Magnus would see that the child was provided what she needed, but the hope of Ollie's reformation was slim to none. Ada, embracing Cissie, thanked her and let her know that when they were successful in their move to San Antonio they would come back and get Laura Bell.

As they returned to the living room, they found Laura Bell seemingly content listing to the music and holding the baby. And so, Ike and Ada departed with some assurance that the little girl they had nurtured over the years was okay with another caring and concerned aunt.

Late afternoon the Woods family arrived in San Antonio. Ike had followed exactly his sister Ellen's instruction on how to get to her home. When they stopped in front of the house, both Ada and Ike were amazed at its vastness and its beauty in pristine white with breathtaking columns as they marveled at the magnificent veranda.

Ellen had been fortunate in her domestic work to work for a millionaire White couple who had provided, rather than service quarters on their property, a beautiful house in the midst of a Negro community of upscale residents. There was a teacher next door, a doctor and police officer across the street and a Pullman Porter and headwaiter around the corner. Ada, who had been the sole woman in her own house knew in her heart that she could only stay in Ellen's home, despite her generous welcome, for a short time.

Ada kept pressuring upon Ike to get a house if they were going to stay in San Antonio. He would always reply in the affirmative, but he needed a job with an income that would sustain them. He was waiting to hear from the Board of Civil Service Examiners. He had taken a test October 16, 1935 for the position of Classified Labor at Fort Sam Houston, Texas. His notice of rating was not good. He had a Disability Preference of 82.0 and his relative denial read in part: "Your relative standing on the list of eligibility is at present number 23. All honorably discharged soldiers, sailors, and marines, and the widows of such, and the wives of injured soldiers, sailors, and marines who themselves are not qualified but whose wives are qualified to hold such positions, are entitled to preference under the act of July 11, 1919."

Ike was devastated at this information when this wasn't a problem when he joined the army. He was embarrassed to share this denial with Ada, but said he was going to get a job of some kind in the city. He was also going to apply to the Veterans Administration for compensation. He did and was awarded a monthly compensation of $30.00. He just needed a little more than this to get a house and maintain it.

CHAPTER 26

Pure Innocence

Now the two little girls—Wee Wee and Agnes Ellen whose nickname was 'Nupie' had no inhibitions and became great playmates. They had turned 5 years' old and was enrolled in Holy Redeemer Catholic School walking distance traveling west from Ellen's house to Nevada, Vargas and Gevers streets.

Ada had taught Wee Wee to read and on this quick recognition by her teacher, Wee Wee was placed in the second grade where she had no competition except in the handwriting discipline. At five years she lacked the motor skills for making those perfect circles and the up and down strokes, and she was rather frustrated about it. But the nun that was her teacher put her at ease because she knew the little girls was very talented.

The first couple of days the girls observed what the other children were eating. They didn't have biscuits with some kind of meat placed in the middle of the biscuit, and a piece of cake or cookies. The second day they were too embarrassed to open their lunch baskets, and did not eat. They did not throw the food away, but took their full baskets back home and placed them on the counter top. When Ada discovered the uneaten food, she questioned them. Quickly Wee Wee blurted out that all the children have sandwiches made with white bread and ham, and they had some fruit. That's the kind of lunch we want. Nupie Agreed. That night Ada shared this information with Ellen. Ellen stated that she would make sandwiches for them before she left for work so that they would not feel less than the other children. She would bring the meat and bread from work because there was more than enough there for sandwiches for two small girls. And so it was. Ada bought cookies and fruit for their lunches.

In the evening after school, the little girls would go next door to Mrs. Mattie Terrell's house where they were taught special dance moves such as "Here We Go Loop Tee Loop." Mrs, Terrell, a public school teacher, marveled at the efforts of Wee Wee the tiny one and Nupie the fat one. She had no children of her own, and apparently these two little girls filled that gap.

CHAPTER 27

An Undesirable Decision

In an evening conversation on the veranda with Mr. Daddy he told Ike about how some Negro young men were working in the downtown hotels and some bars as bartenders.

After several weeks of Ike's efforts to find a job, Ada decided that she and the baby needed to go back to Rockdale and stay until Ike found a job. Knowing her desire, Ike convinced her to stay until the school year ended so that their little girl's education would not be interrupted—thinking about his own lack of education. Ada realizing his valid point about the child was worthy of her consent to stay.

After the last day of school, Ike knowing his wife and understanding her need of independence in her home experiences kept his promise. He had enough money to buy a train ticket for her and to send Barney a telegram about Ada and the baby returning. "Please pick them up at the station on time" was the plea on the telegram. Faithful Barney was there at the station to take them home when they arrived. As they traveled to the house, Barney asked about Ike because he was concerned about his health; however, he was careful not to make it a big issue. And he asked her about Ellen. Although Ada, too, was concerned about Ike's health she, also, was cautious to set up an alarm. She hesitated a bit about Ellen, telling about her beautiful home, her devotion and work habit in her daily service to the people she worked for. She talked about how she would bring enough food home for supper for her family and her live-in companion family member called Mr. Daddy. There was no explanation for the name brand for this very tall dark-skinned Wartuse—Clan-looking man who had a sinister appearance, but in truth was a likeable person who had the strange habit of over salting anything he had to eat. Ada conceded that her sister-in-law was hospitable to her and her child, but she knew she could not, they could not have a long-time stay in Ellen's home. It was more about how each filled their role as homemakers. In reality there didn't appear to be a lot of joy in the family.

CHAPTER 28

Back Home

Ada was relieved when she walked into her house and saw how well Barney had kept up the place even the kitchen. She let him know how much she appreciated his interest in the up keep of the property by baking him her favorite cake that he always enjoyed.

After a couple of days at home, even after attending church services and the love greetings of her neighbors, Ada missed her husband. She missed the caress of his arms in the morning as they lay there in the past talking about their dreams and hopes for a better day. Tears began to well up in her eyes, but when she saw her little girl coming in to get in the bed with her, she thought about her blessings in this now healthy visible child. She took her in her arms and kissed her several times. Wee Wee looked at her mama and wondered why there was a tear coming down her cheek.

A week passed with Ada concerned about not receiving a letter or a telegram from Ike. June 22, 1936 she received an unexpected, unneeded letter from her youngest brother Onie who was now in Fort Worth, Texas. Ada had no idea why this young nomadic brother was there. The content and purpose of his letter was that he knew Ike had received his bonus from the government and he needed Ada to send him $2.00. Ada was truly upset with this request knowing that they needed all the money Ike could get to start a new life in San Antonio. But frugal as Ada was, she had enough from her baking and eggs sales that she was able reluctantly to send him the $2.00. She did not receive a 'thank you' in return.

In San Antonio, Ike's persistence in applying in several places as Mr. Daddy had suggested and encouraged him to, landed him a job at a place called The Wonder Bar. He was employed as a bartender. His gregarious personality and back-home memory of his 'Goliath's Blood' and how he excited customers with his cheerful behavior paid off in this genre. He was liked and respected by his employer and caused increased sales by the nightly patrons.

He found a house to rent, but knew it had to be furnished, and that certainly had to include the move of furnishings from Rockdale and any new furnishings that had to be bought. And so he felt the need to write Ada and hope she still wanted him and would return to San Antonio forgiving him of this long time without communicating.

Ada was distraught because every day Barney brought the mail to the house there was no letter from Ike. In the month of August, among the pieces of mail Barney brought home was the following letter:

August 26, 1936

Mrs. Ada Woods Dearest little wife and sweet little Wee Wee

I hope this letter will find both of you well. I am not doing any good at all. Ada I been sick about two weeks but just wouldn't give up. Ada I know you wondered what is the matter. Ada you really too good for me and I been 'shamed to meet you face to face. Ada you don't know how blue I am and shame had the truck ready to come after the things last Monday as promi'sd you. Went down and forgot all about what I was supposed to do and that' not all. Oh I am not any good and you believe me I am not enuff for you and the baby. When you see me you will find out. Now if you still want to come to me anser right back. I have still got the house and would send for the things. I no dear you have worried and cryed about the way I have did so don't worry and cry about me. I am not worth it. I just haven' any business thought. But from now on I am gong to put you at the head of everything. O I haven't got sense at all you see if you ever see me again. Kiss the baby. Tell her I can't sleep now for thinking about you both. I no she wont to see her crazy no good daddy, so if you want to come to me 'rite me right back but I am not worth it. Guess you wonder why I talk like I am, really Ada I am 'shame sending you a little money. After doing so bad, I thought I had better find out if you wanted to come back over here. Must close be sweet. I have'n got 'nuff sense to rite what I wont to.

Your Ike

PS Ada ask Barney to give you Robbies address and Ruby and when you rite me again send it to me. Get the things all up. Rite me if you haven't sold anything. Well you may sell the icebox. How is the baby? Is she about ready to come back? Not able to clean up the house. I'll go clean it up some time this week. Well I guess I will hafter to stop here. Kiss Wee Wee for me. Tell Pig I said I drink my job up. Ha. ha. I no thats what he think. Love to all. Your hubby.

Ada cried with joy as she read Ike's letter to her. She had a feeling he had been sick because it was discovered when he had a physical exam at Ft. Sam Houston Hospital by Medical Assistant Lenore F. Paschal, that he had a serious hernia defect. But she was overjoyed to know their love for each other was still strong—unchanging.

Immediately she commissioned Barney to help her in determining what furniture to take, because she knew Barney was going to remain in the homestead. Barney borrowed a truck from a close friend and with the help of Ralph and Willie Goins, whose family was also moving to San Antonio, loaded the bedroom, living room and dining room furniture on the truck. Ada devised a container to take several of her chickens including the important rooster. Little Wee Wee was excited even though she really didn't know what was happening except that she was going to take a long ride back to the place where she was going to have to go to school again.

Late afternoon on a sunshiny day they arrived in San Antonio stopping at Ellen's house. Ike grabbed Ada, lifting her from her feet planting kisses all over her face and then he picked up his little girl giving her a big bear hug and also kisses. The little girl looked at her father with her big brown eyes, cupping his face with her tiny little hands and planted a big smack on his check. Laughter erupted from those watching.

Ellen had prepared lunch for all. The conversation at the table was primarily Ike talking about the house he had rented from a Mr. Jacob and his daughter Anna Bell Levine and her husband. Mr. Jacob, described by Ike, as a little old Jew man who had several rent houses and a multipurpose building in the area where Negro families, some Mexican families and an indigent White family with the last name of Peters that had an adult mentally challenged son named Jack lived.

After lunch and Ada's cleaning the kitchen, they journeyed to the house Ike had rented. It was in walking distance from Ellens house, three grocery stores, a drug store in the Jacob's building and four churches—one Methodist, one Baptist, and two Catholic. In addition were two beauty shops, one Negro owned restaurant and one Negro owned Barbecue Pit and a tavern. These establishments and the residents defined this eastside residential area three miles from the downtown area.

When Ada saw the house, she was awed overwhelmingly by its newness and its beauty. It wasn't as large as the home place in Rockdale, but it had a bedroom, a living room, dining room, kitchen, an extra room and a front and back porch. There was a deep rectangular back yard where an outhouse stood in its midst. Ada could see the potential for her garden and chicken coup.

Following them to the house was Mr. Daddy who helped Ike and Barney unload the truck.

CHAPTER 29

Another Start

The Ike Woods family seemed to settle in their new home and getting acquainted with their cultural and race mix. Next door on the West was the Gonzales family. Mr. Gonzales operated a barbershop and a small grocery store that occupied the front portion of their home. And they had two shot-gun rent houses in the back yard area. They had two adult daughters, Ada learned from other neighbors, who were sent to Mexico every summer hoping they would come home engaged to be are already married. Unfortunately in all the years they were sent it never happened. Now Mrs. Gonzales, their mother, spoke no English. Ada spoke no Spanish, but they became best of friends sharing their culinary expertise. Ada's cakes especially the orange/ lemon frosted cake and the pound cake, and Mrs. Gonzales' pork tamales (whose meat inside a masa ingredient and rolled in a prepared corn shuck came from a hogs head) a first taste experience for Ada and Ike. And her cheese enchiladas and beef crispy tacos were a delightful experience for Ada.

Next door on the east was the Waiters family—Gertrude who must have been a descendent of one who had been a victim of miscegenation. She could have passed as 'White.' Her husband Rufus was all Negro in both dark complexion and facial features. Their young son 'Jr.' the age of Wee Wee had Gertrude's complexion, hair and facial features. Next door to the Waiters was a single Mexican young mother with a small son named Otavia. And next door to this family was a very unusual family—an elderly White man married to a young dark-skinned Mexican woman. They had four sons and one daughter who was the youngest of the children. This was the biracial Witherspoon family. In view from the

Wood's resident two streets across directly facing the Wood's house was the White Peters family that had a mentally challenged adult son. One of the unique things in this home was green onions. As one would have fruit on the table in a bowl, this family had green onions. Jack, the son, would as often as he desired take and eat as if he were eating a piece of fruit. Other Negro families on the same street as the Peters were the Blounts—a matriarch of daughters and their children. Only one of the daughters had a husband. Directly across the street going west were the Ellisons the Cottons and the Malones—a matriarch with daughter and her son who was 2 years younger than Wee Wee. From Montana Street north, Walters Street east, Nebraska Street south and New Braunfels Street West was the demographic composition of this eastside community. Walking distance from the Woods home were the White owned Dierolf grocery store, the Mexican owned Marie's grocery store and the Chinese owned grocery store. There were three popular Negro cafes—"Clydes" full service with barbecue at the corner of New Braunfels Ave. and Montana Street, Kriss' Restaurant at the corner of Gevers and Hedges and Mr. Washington's Barbecue place behind his resident on Hedges Street. Elementary school children from Holy Redeemer Catholic School frequented this place to purchase his popular sausage served with two slices of white bread. This very small barbecue place had walls as black as the complexion of the over weight Mr. Washington. And there was Warner's Tavern situated between Marie's grocery store on the east and Jacob Chapels United Methodist Church on the west. All facing Hedges Street. East of Dierolf's grocery store on the south side of Hedges Street were the two sisters' Beauty shop. They did great transformations of the Negro women in the community who used their services to straighten and curl their hair. It was a daily six-days-a-week-business for the sisters.

Ada and Ike felt very comfortable in this mix of human diversion, and Wee Wee had neighborhood children to play with.

The couple really liked their rental house, but Ike had one thing he desperately wanted to do. He wanted to have an indoor bathroom like his sister Ellen had. And, he wanted to tear down the outhouse in the back yard. But, he knew, with his small monthly pension and his unpredictable income from his bartenders' job it would take awhile to have enough money to get this needed project done. It was a goal he intended to accomplish.

With circumstances as they were, the family settled in, happy about their new resident, thankful that the family was still in walking distance from Ike's sister's home, and a very short distance from Holy Redeemer School that Wee Wee attended.

Now this was not the greatest venture for tiny Wee Wee. She didn't have her plump cousin Nupie to walk to school with her. Ada in her protective nature took up this baton. But she would walk only to Marie's grocery store where she could watch Wee Wee travel the block and a half and enter the schoolyard. This was not an acceptable solution for little Wee Wee. And so for three days strait, she would turn around crying uncontrollably causing a scene at the corner of Hedges and Vargas streets. And she followed Ada as she started returning home. Ada was embarrassed as the store keeper, beauticians, street walkers came out to find out what was happening. Ada realizing the onlookers concern would take Wee Wee by the hand and walk all the way to the school grounds. The third day, Ada thought enough is enough, and when her tiny daughter whom she loved unconditionally came home, she waited particularly until she pulled off her school clothes to put on her play clothes. Now Ada had already secured a switch from the peach tree, and with Wee Wee between the bed and the wall, Ada began the whipping process on Wee Wee's seat of correction. All the time she is hurting more than the child but remembering the book of Ecclesiastic's verse "Spare the rod and spoil the child." But, Ada realized she had made a few too many swatches for the child had a few visible whelps on her tiny thighs. Seeing this, Ada immediately picked her up hugged and kissed her while the tears flowed from both the doer and the receiver. Ada feared what Ike might say when he saw the tiny whelps on the child when he and his Rockdale, Lexington and new San Antonio friends returned from hunting—Ikes favorite past time. Ada quickly went into the small room that was to be the future modern bathroom, pulled the galvanized tin tub down, poured the boiling water from the kettle mixing it with enough cold water to be just warm enough to put the child in hoping this would cause the few visible whelps to dissipate. And so little Wee Wee had her moment of correction as well as nightly baths early. Neither talked about the incident as Ada prepared dinner with Wee Wee watching her and setting the table as Ada had taught her.

That night in bed, Ada felt so guilty and she knew she would never do it again, tearfully she told Ike what had happened. She just didn't know the solution to this ongoing daily problem. Ike took her gently in his arms and said, "I'll walk her to school until she feels safe and traveling with other children that are in the neighborhood. What Ike and Ada came to realize was the fact that most of the Negro children in the area attended Cuney Elementary Negro (separate but equal so the state claimed) public school. Wee Wee and Nupie were enrolled in Holy Redeemer Parochial School whose teachers were nuns from Louisiana. The school was defined as a Grammar School operating under the 0-9th grade plan. Children started in the pre-primer class and progressed through the ninth grade.

Now the nuns at Holy Redeemer had an affinity for this tiny little girl given the full name of Dolores Maxine Woods. They recognized at her early age she was gifted and they tried to pacify her during her crying spells by taking her to the small children's dining area and serving her shaved ice in a paper cup with flavored sweet juice poured over it. They explained to Ada that she would soon get over her fears, and they allowed Ada to pick her up each day after lunch for a month. This lack of a full day in school did not affect the child's acquisition of things taught in her absence. Ada did what one would say was unauthorized home schooling during the afternoon teaching periods. Ada and Ike were pleased that the child was being taught Christian values as every child in parochial schools had catechism classes daily.

When Wee Wee had problems with her math homework for some reason she didn't believe her parents could help her, so ritualistically having been trained to pray and ask God for what she needed, she would kneel and pray silently and place her book under her pillow. After seeing her doing this on a few occasions, Ada asked her why she was doing this to which she said matter-of-factly, "I just have a problem that was kinder hard, and so I pray to God for help because I know he knows everything." Ada wanted to laugh out loud, but she controlled this emotional outburst and said, "I'm so happy that you're learning about God's power and His goodness, but you know what? God has given your father a great deal of knowledge about math, and you can ask him also. In a very simplistic manner Wee Wee responded, "OK."

As things seemed to be coming to a normal living pace, bad news crept up. Ada received information that her younger sister Paulena called "Lena" had passed September 8, 1936. The sad thing about it was a sudden death due to Lena's attempt to satisfy her husband who didn't want any more children. Lena became pregnant. Her attempt to abort the fetus was to use a coat hanger as a surgical instrument to do the necessary procedure. The process was a deadly failure. Complete poisoning of her body set in causing immediate death.

CHAPTER 30

The Cat In The Drama

As the nuns at Holy Redeemer School prepared for a dramatic presentation, selecting cast members, little Dolores was cast in the leading role of a cat. When she brought the script home and showed it to Ada, she remembered her own failed effort and embarrassment when she walked off the pulpit without saying a word as a high school student. The next day Ada went to the school to let the sisters know that the part of the cat was too much for her child to memorize. Wee Wee was not a part of the conference, and did not know her mother came to bargain with the nuns to give her a lessor part. Wee Wee's language teacher broke in saying, "Oh no Mrs. Woods! She can do it. You have a very talented little daughter, and we have no doubt that she can do it." She went on to say, "But she has to have a costume. Do you think you might be able to furnish that?" Ada, conceding her efforts to remove her child from possible embarrassment, she said simply, "I think so." And with her designing and sewing talent, immediately she found a picture of a cat, drew a design, and used an old gray nightgown for the material. She didn't need much material for her tiny little girl's costume. The next day when Wee Wee came home from school, she had her step into the costume that covered her body from head to toe with a long stuffed tail placed strategically in the right place. It was a perfect fit.

When Ike came inside he burst out laughing seeing how much she looked like a little cat with the whiskers and all. He picked her up, kissed her and said, "You're the prettiest and greatest little kitten in the world. Hugging her daddy, Wee Wee blurted out, "You're just saying that daddy.

You know I'm not a cat." Ada and Ike looking at each other laughing and realizing the knowledge of reality the child had. As predicted the play was a success and Wee Wee did a superstar performance. Many of the other parents came up to congratulate Ike and Ada for their child's superb performance.

CHAPTER 31

Life in the Big City

Settling in their new residence, Ike and Ada began communicating with their Rockdale hometown friends—the Goins, Mitchells, Lewis and Lexington friends—the Taylors, Ada's cousins—the Joiners (five of the 19 children in that family) and their new friends—the Waiters, the Mitchells, Julia Eto and a significant group of church members who embraced the young couple. Ike learned of and met a nephew he didn't know. He was a child his 'jack-leg, nomadic' preacher brother Jessie had sired with a young woman who chose not give him the Woods last name, but her own—Lewis. And so she named the boy Joe Lewis. This young man now in his mid 20's was an honorably discharged sailor who now worked for the government. For some reason he took a special affinity for Ada and made a lot of visits to his uncle's house.

With his home buddies, Ike in his days off during the appropriate season went hunting and Ada occasionally would go fishing with her cousins. And so, life that seemed serene for the Woods family was not as it seemed. Ike was a sick young man having been diagnosed with a chronic heart condition and a double hernia.

The year 1938 was a trying year for the couple. Ike's sister Ellen died. Ada received a letter from her sister Ollie stating that Laura Bell wanted to visit them and she would be in San Antonio the following day. Ada remembered what she had promised Laura Bell that she would send for her when they settled. But quite a few years had gone by. So, Ada was happy about her coming. What she didn't know was that 19-year old Laura Bell was pregnant.

Ada was shocked when she saw Laura Bell's condition, and she was angry not at Laura Bell but her sister Ollie who didn't mention anything about her pregnancy. The family welcomed Laura Bell and set her up in their added room behind the indoor bathroom that had been installed. Despite her condition Laura Bell felt safe and truly cared for by her aunt and uncle.

In the evening following supper, three days after Laura's arrival, Ada complained about a pain in her side. She didn't sleep. When Ike woke up the next morning he took her against her wishes to the hospital. He did the right thing for she had a tumor that required surgery. By family and friends' prayers, physician expertise, the surgery was a success. In this surgery procedure, however, her doctors were simply perplexed that she did not wake up when she should have. In fact as they checked her, she had no heartbeat or pulse, and in a physician's assessment she was dead. For some reason the senior physician could not accept this declaration, did not send her to the morgue and posted a nurse to watch her until he returned. After exactly one hour, the nurse saw her squirming and heard her say in a strong voice, "I went away, but I came back." The nurse quickly called the doctors in who were completely astonished but immediately began wrapping her legs from ankle through her thighs to booster her circulation.

Four days later Ada was at home doing what she did best—being a wife, a mother and a homemaker. No one asked her what she meant when she came to and made that strange statement. They were just profoundly happy that she didn't stay wherever her out-of-body experience was.

Soon after things seemed normal in the household an unexpected tragedy occurred. Ike had gone hunting with his friends in seemingly good physical condition, but the noise Ada heard outside from the men she knew something was wrong. Running to the front door, she saw the men carrying Ike and calling out, "Ada! Ike needs to go to the hospital, he can't walk and his speech is blurred." Mustering her strength, fearing the worst, she ordered, "Put him back in the car, we have to take him to the Fort Sam Houston government hospital. Let me get my purse." The hospital was less than three miles from their home. She instructed Laura Bell to take care of Wee Wee keep her in the house and to give her supper she had already prepared.

At the hospital the senior doctor informed Ada that Ike had suffered a life-changing experience. He had suffered a stroke and was paralyzed on the left side. He predicted that this would not change, but believed his ability to speak coherently would be restored in time.

Ada found no opportunity to go into a state of depression. She had to be strong, and take control of matters she had no need to be concerned with previously.

Financially the family was truly in a bind. In a few weeks, Laura's baby was going to be born—another expense. She realized that Ike's small $30.00 monthly pension was not enough.

Although a May 13, 1938 Letter from the S.A. Veterans' Administration signed by Adjudication Officer J. H. Skinner said in part: "We are pleased to acknowledge the receipt of a certified copy of the public record of your marriage, which evidence is formed to be in proper form and the same has been filed as a part of the permanent record in your claim," Ike's pension was not increased. Ada knew as she thumbed through Ike's military papers from the United States Civil Service Commission Board October 16, 1935 after applying for a laborers job he had a disability preference of 82.0—a notch above the 70 percent requirement and he was #23 on the list of eligible applicants. But, he was never hired, and now Ada realized it would be useless for him to ever apply again. She concluded that the rent from Barney in the home place in Rockdale was not enough either, and they needed to sell the house.

When Ike came home, she would find an appropriate time to talk about the matter. She also knew his bartending job at the Wonder Bar was over. The owner who liked Ike a great deal, was truly devastated by his physical condition and had compassion for the family knowing the financial stress they no doubt were having. He did what he had never done for an employee who left the job. Charging it to his Christian family background, he presented Ike a sizable severance pay. It was enough to tide them through at least three months.

Ike being released from the hospital and coming home, he did not have an opportunity to have a pity party because he had this curious little daughter who did not accept this now inability her father was experiencing and insisted he help her wash the dishes after supper. The little girl was his heart and knowing this was an impossible task. But, she had a system figured out. She sat on his lap—the left-afflicted leg, and she would hold the dishes that he would wash with his working right hand and arm. Ada thought it was therapeutic and laughed as she watched.

Laura Bell didn't join this happy household venture because she realized her pregnancy was about to come to an end. November 24, 1938 Laura Bell gave birth to a beautiful baby girl. Eight-year old Wee Wee had successfully made a dress at school where girls were taught at this tender age to sew using the old foot treadle sewing machine. It was a beautiful little garment, and Ada was proud of her little girl thinking 'the apple doesn't fall too far from the tree' and thinking of her own sewing ability.

Laura Bell and Ada agreed on the name Wee Wee suggested—Laura Louise. Because Laura bell was not a raving beauty, friends who came over to see the baby on their behavior and facial countenance looked at the baby and at Laura Bell in disbelief.

The Woods family fell in love with this new resident, and she became the second apple in Ike's eyes. In private when Ada asked Laura Bell who the father was, Laura Bell told her Gary Taylor in Lexington, Texas. Now Ada rationalized that when Laura Bell was sent to her grandmother Isabel for a brief visit while her mother Ollie was gallivanting in Temple and neighboring towns, she probably had a one-night stand with Gary. However Ada, a discerning adult saw another resemblance that was more striking. It was the likeness of her baby sister Fannie's husband Gus. The baby had his fair complexion, his hairline, his hair texture and facial contour. Ada had no doubt and she shared her belief with Ike who looked at the child with greater attention agreed with her, but they never told Laura Bell what they felt.

CHAPTER 32

The Perpetual Storm

Nineteen thirty-nine was a competitive year for the family—almost a replica of 1938. Ike realized his physical handicap and his inability to do any kind of labor work, felt he needed once again to appeal to the Veterans Administration for the granting of an increased monthly pension. He knew that he needed a doctor's evaluation of his extreme handicap condition. December 4, 1939 he sought the services of Dr. A. Graves. After a thorough examination, Dr. Graves provided a letter to the state of Texas, County of Bexar in which he wrote:

I, Dr. A. Graves Sr., a resident of San Antonio, Bexar County, Texas, after being duly deposes and says: I am a licensed physician, having practiced medicine for a period of 47 years I am acquainted with one Isaac Woods who resides at 2007 Wyoming St. in San Antonio, Texas, a World War II Veteran.

I have known Isaac Woods for a period of three or four years. I had occasion to treat and examine Isaac Woods on or about November 15, 1939. He came to my office and requested an examination to determine his condition, and extent of his disability. At that time he complained to be suffering from several ailments. I made a thorough examination as was possible in the time I took him over. I found from my examination that he was suffering as follows:

Myocardial infarction with hypertension systolic 220, irregular pulse, loss of control of sphincter and from an operation in the Ball Hospital in Fort Riley Kansas in 1918 he also had double inguinal hernias.

Conclusion: From the forging findings it is my conclusion that Isaac Woods is totally and permanently disabled, and is wholly unable to perform physical labor.

Apparently a non-military doctor's findings were insufficient for the veteran administration to take action, so the VA required that Ike travel to the veterans' hospital for examination by a military doctor. This need was expressed in the December 5, 1939 letter that stated:

Dear Sir:

This is to acknowledge receipt of statement by Dr. Amos Graves Sr. reporting your present physical condition.

As soon as your hospital report from Alexander Louisiana can be secured, your claim will be considered and you will be notified of the action taken with reference to your entitlement to an increase in your compensation.

By Director,
S. P. Kohen
Adjudication Officer

The message in the letter was most discouraging to Ike. He couldn't understand why the diagnosis of a qualified civilian medical doctor was not accepted. Ada, trying to influence Ike to have a positive attitude about the situation, she shared that she wouldn't worry about that, the army always felt they had the real experts on everything and she encouraged Ike to go with the idea that some good would come from the trip. Ada's faith and belief in the healing ability of her maker caused her to spend a much longer time in prayer that evening.

The next morning Ike made it known that he was going to Alexandria, Louisiana because he needed to get an increase in his monthly pension. But, he would not be going right away.

In the mean time, Laura Bell secured what would be a lifetime job in the downtown Graysons store whose merchandise and prices served the blue-collar worker and the under privileged. She started out as a presser. Ada was proud of her niece and the fact that she was able to provide resources for household expenses and for the needs of her child. Laura

Bell's permanent job at the Grayson department store and contribution to household fixed expenses were helpful to Ada as she now had the full responsibility for budget balancing.

January 1940 Ike traveled by train to Alexandria, Louisiana for the examination—a daring experience for a paraplegic. Examination results were not financially encouraging. In fact, they were depressing. A January 13, 1940 document signed by Adjudication Officer S.P. Kohen in part stated: ". . . The decision rendered was the effect that no material change was found in your service connected condition that would warrant a change in your current rating of 10%. Accordingly, in view of the action taken, you will continue to receive your award of non-service pension as the greater benefit at the rate of $30.00 per month as heretofore until further notice."

CHAPTER 33

Invisible Courtship

Ike's nephew Joe became a constant visitor to Ike's house. He was allowed to take Wee Wee to baseball games where every time he had a beer he thought the child should have another Hippo Soda Water of her choice. The child, thinking as an adult, knew one bottle of this giant sweet drink was more than sufficient. So she never drank more than one bottle.

Little did Ada know about the invisible courtship of Ike's nephew Joe and her niece Laura Bell. Joe was 11 years older than Laura Bell. That did not seem to be a factor in their courtship. After five months of this invisible courtship, Laura Bell told her aunt that she was getting married. And what Laura Bell thought was a secret was surprised when Ada said, "I think Joe will make a fine husband for you. What would you like me to do?"

Laura Bell knowing her aunts financial situation assured her that she didn't have to do anything because she and Joe were going to have a brief ceremony at the court house. Joe had secured a practically new two-bedroom house on Center Street close enough for Ada to walk to. However, they had to stay at Ada's house for three months before the house was ready for occupancy. Ada was truly happy for her niece and her little daughter Laura Louise.

Ike's tenure in the hospital did not yield hope or satisfaction regarding his becoming a well and pain free person. July 9, 1940 he writes to Ada:

Mrs. Ada Woods dear wife,

This will let you know how I am today. I am not feeling good am still in bed and don't know how long I will be in bed.

I rec'd your letter and have intended to answer before now but feeling bad is why I put it off. Hope you are still doing fine and all is well. You must pardon my delay.

I heard the ball game over the radio lying down and if I had been out I would of lost on the American League because I thought sure it would have won.

Ada I have not been able to be out since being here over two months never had that happen before in my whole life, but I guess everything will work out after while. It seems I will have to stop talking about coming home. How is my baby? Kiss her for me. My arm is not getting no better. Now I did not know mother-in-law sent the shoes. Anyway I certainly appreciate them. It was really fine for her. Now don't stop writing because I'm a little long in answering because you know how it is with me. Tell me about the entire family and all my inquiring friends. How much do you charge Laura Bell and Joe for rent and how much do Doltha pay for Vunsil. And did she tell you she was going to send for her. Please explain the questions in your next letter. Now I will close. Don't forget to tell me what Joe and them is paying you.

Love to you
Your husband Isaac Woods

In her new letter to Ike, Ada shared that she had not charged Joe and Laura Bell anything, but Joe had given her more than she would have asked for. Joe had secured a nice house on Center Street and they were moving in a couple of months when it was ready. Their moving would allow her to have another room to rent.

The United States entering in the World War II 12/7/1941 as a result of Japan's attack on Pearl Harbor caused a military growth in San Antonio. Ada had an opportunity whenever she had a vacant room or rear apartment vacancy there was a young military couple or single person to rent one of the vacancies.

Reading the letter, Ada was happy and sad. Happy to hear from him but sad and feeling emotionally his pain and suffering. In a rare instance she began to cry. She loved her husband so much, but by his words she feared he had little chance of getting well. Ada knew as she read the letter he was unable to write it. Someone had been kind enough to write as he dictated. The clue was the handwriting and the spelling, and particularly the signature. She knew he would not sign Isaac Woods, but simply 'Ike.'

Ike was hurt but not surprised by the decision of the Veterans Administration. In his letter following this depressing information, he said to Ada, "It's okay honey. We'll make it. I'm going to sell some more property in Rockdale and ask Barney for a couple more dollars on his rent. I know he won't object." Trying to put Ada's fears to rest he wrote about this second term president Franklin Delano Roosevelt, a rich guy, a tragic victim of polio causing him to loose the use of his legs and the fact that he did something no other president had. He talked to the people using the radio as the means in what he called "Fireside" chats. Ike wanted Ada to believe that this president was going to do something about situations like his because he believed the things he talked about and this "New Deal" which will help a lot of people who need work. Ada reading his long diatribe to the end internally shared his views because of how she had been raised to believe that people had to work for what ever they needed and not expect hand outs from others. But she was in agreement that the government needed to help soldiers who had risked their lives and died to protect us. And their families should receive benefits as a result of death or injuries causing permanent disability. On this note, her political thoughts ended.

CHAPTER 34

Before the Dusk

August 6, 1940 Ike received a Veterans Administration Medical Form 2512 which was a Travel Authorization in Facility Discharge document. He was discharged from the hospital on his way home with no change in his physical challenges and pain. To make the journey the document authorized him to receive Railroad Fare of $8.93 and 2 meals—$1.00 (.50 each)

Upon his arrival home in San Antonio, family members struggled to avoid the depression and sorrow they felt about the physical condition and possible demise of the head of the family. Ada, having developed friends with many church members and their knowledge of her sewing ability, she had a steady income from designing and sewing new garments for them or altering others to fit properly.

For enjoyment and leisure activities Ike's friends would come by and take him with them on their hunting ventures. Ada went fishing when she could. At a one-time venture trying to climb over a fence to get to the fishing hole she was almost kissed by a snake hanging from the tree above the fence. This curtailed her fishing for awhile, and she did not share this glorious experience with Ike.

Laura Bell occasionally took her baby and Wee Wee to Lincoln Park at the east end of Commerce Street to swing and watch softball games. Sometimes they went to the Cameo Theatre—the Negro theatre on Commerce near the downtown area. This area was where Negro entrepreneurs owned restaurants, stores and hotels. Cousan Lemelle, a Creole from Louisiana, was one of the hotel owners. He was married to Birdie Frank of an affluent Negro family. Popular establishments were The Life Saver noted for its' breakfast parties attended by prominent social organizations; Froggy Bottom—a place of various questionable activities and the Avalon Grill a building of a street floor and a second floor capacity where dancing and other activities took place.

Tragedy was in the loom, however, for the Ike Woods family. While preparing dinner Ada heard the speed of cars and the abrupt stopping in from of the house. Knowing something was wrong, and fearing the worst, she ran to the door to see two robust men carrying Ike. Not knowing his condition, Ada commanded the men to put him back in the car, that he had to go to the hospital. They didn't hesitate in turning around, and Ada grabbing her purse, got in the car with him. Although Ike was unconscious, Ada had hope because he had a heart beat, when she didn't after her surgery but was yet alive to tell the story. As Ada prayed silently and thought about her marriage during the 1930's through the 1941 year. October 20, 1934 Elizabeth her mother's only full sister passed. September 8, 1936 as have been mentioned was Paulina's (Lena) death. September 8, 1937 her protector, beloved and mentally challenged big brother Bud passed. And here she was this hour waiting for a decision from the doctors at this Fort Sam Houston Medical Center Looking up with hopeful anticipation as she watched the doctor approach them. Examination by the physician, the specialist who attended Ike, yielded grim but decisive news—that being at 11:30 p.m., January 18, 1941, Ike passed.

CHAPTER 35

A Celebration of Life

They came from Rockdale, Lexington, Cameron and Temple, all Texas towns—life long friends, family and in-laws. From Rockdale came the Wratts, the Arnwines, and the Goins loyal and caring friends. Ada's cousins Amelia and Zillie Joiner from Austin of the 17 Joiner cousins and three of whom lived in San Antonio, Texas. Old and new friends and relatives totaled 150 people who attended this emotional but silent celebration of life of a man who was admired by many. Especially did they admire the love and affection for each other demonstrated by the young couple.

There was somberness in the church as the family entered. Silent tears were abundant as members watched the young mother and ten-year old daughter walk down the aisle to be seated.

The order of service was brief—The invocation, a congregational hymn, old and New Testament scripture reading and the eulogy. Most impressive was the reading of the obituary written and delivered by lifetime friend Willie B. Wratt from Rockdale. She titled it "Obituary Biography of Isaac Hannibal Woods." There was complete silence as she read:

> Sadly we sing with tremorless breath as we
> Stand by the mystic stream
> In the dark valley and
> Shadow of death and yet
> 'tis no more than a dream
>
> Whereas it has pleased almighty
> God to come into

Our midst and take
From us our own
Friend and companion
Isaac Hannibal Woods, we
Can only bow our heads in
humble submission to Him
Who doeth all things well.
It has been once appointed
That all men must die. Every
Knee must bow and every
Tongue confess and the
Body return to its mother
Dust and the soul to the
God that giveth.
Our lives are like the autumn
Rose that opens to the
Morning sky, but ere the
Shades of evening close
Is scattered to the earth die.
Ike, we hoped, tried to work out
His own souls salvation
With fear and trembling

Isaac Hannibal Woods was
Born in Milam County, Rockdale,
Texas June 2, 1894.
He was the son of John and
Ellen Woods who departed
This life years ago. He spent
All his boyhood and nearly
All of his young manhood
Days in Rockdale. He was
A member of New Hope
Baptist Church Rockdale.
Was married to Miss
Ada Green at Ballenger,
Texas 1920. He served
Well his part in the

World's war. Born to
Their union one child.
Moved to San Antonio and
Joined Shiloh
Baptist church under the
Pastorate of Rev. S.E. Steward.
Isaac's health has been
Failing him for several
years. Medical attention
Given but all was in
Vain. To know it was to
Love him. He was a kind
Compassionate friend.
He has lived by the side of
The road and been a friend
To many a man. He was
Jolly and always full of glee
He passed January 18, 1941, 11:30 p,.m.
At Fort Sam Houston Hospital.
Yes, we will miss him and
You will miss him too
He leaves a darling devoted
Wife, a loving child, 2
Brothers-in-law, sisters-in-law
Other relatives and a host
Of friends to mourn his
Loss. Therefore, we can only
Quote the words of Job.
The Lord giveth and the
Lord taketh away.
Blessed be the name of
The Lord.

The evening at home for Ada was an emotional challenge for her. She needed to cry, but she needed to appear normal for the sake of her child, Laura Bell and her child all of whom she had pretty much a divine affinity for each of them. So Ada had to be brave, and after going far into the back yard out of sight she knelt and prayed to the God Jehovah she served and believed in his mighty power. She asked Him for strength to overcome the loss she had experienced at age 42. And she asked for wisdom and knowledge concerning what she needed to do and the source of help. Ada was a true believer having become a part of the Christian faith and an active member of the neighborhood church called Corinth. She was radiant as she entered the house, travel to the kitchen starting the evening meal. Laura Bell, Wee Wee and the baby secretly (as they thought) peering behind the entrance door to the kitchen. Ada, knowing they were there, in her normal voice told Laura Bell to take the children outside to play with neighborhood children who were always outside—Annie Mae, Joyce, Marcus, Rufus, Nick and Octavia—and she would call them when supper was ready. Convinced that her aunt was herself, Laura Bell took the children outside. She sat on the porch watching them as they played softball in the street.

The following week there was a constant bidding of well wishers—hometown friends and new acquaintances in San Antonio especially those who were members of her church. They brought food, fresh fruit and garden vegetables. Ada had no doubt that her prayers were being answered. Mollie and Mandrew Mitchell, Gussie Thompson and her husband became her closest friends.

Mandrew sensing that Ada lacked knowledge of what to do about her eligibility to receive a government pension from her husband's service in the military informed her what she needed to do. She did as he instructed her to. In the mean time she receives a letter, dated January 20, 1941 undersigned by Lucille B. Pourie, Field Director from the American Red Cross Station Hospital, Fort Sam Houston, Texas in part expressing sympathy for her loss and stating ". . . should you need any assistance with government claims that you telephone Miss Virginia Selby, Home Service Secretary, Bexar County Chapter, American Red Cross, in San Antonio, Texas. Her Telephone number is Fannin 9151 and her office is on the fourth floor of the Court House."

Ada acted swiftly using a neighbor's phone. By phone an interview was scheduled in which she participated. After several days had passed, and with much anticipation, she received a letter from S.P. Kohen, Adjudication Officer, Veteran's Administration dated February 26,1941 which informed her that as the unmarried widow of Isaac Woods, whose death was not due to service, an award of death compensation had been made to her under the provisions of the Act of June 28, 1934, as amended at the monthly rate of $30.00 per month commencing January 19, 1941 and continuing until further notice. They would also consider her minor child Dolores upon her submitting a public record of her birth. Ada complied immediately. March 20, 1941 a communication from the same adjudication officer informed her that her compensation payment had been increased from $30.00 to $38.00 per month commencing the original date of her award January 19, 1941 so as to include her minor child—Dolores Maxine Woods.

Ada was not disturbed that stipulation for receiving these benefits meant that she could not marry. If she did, her compensation would be discontinued. Being involved with any other man was something Ada had no desire for. Ike was still her heartbeat. She missed his caresses, his unexpected kisses and she missed how he would pick her up and dance around the room when she was fussing about something he did or did not do. The loneliness was like a deep cut that was going to take a long time to heal. But when she looked at her little girl, she had to focus on the future for her sake. For this reason and having learned about the cost for funeral services and burials, she felt it necessary to do something for her little girl. November 17, 1942 she took out from the Juvenile Department of the Grand Court of Calantha of Texas Jurisdiction #2069 Sirus B. a Burial Certificate for her eleven-year-old daughter. It had a value of $50.00 the first year of membership, $75.00 the second year of membership and $100.00 the third year of membership.

Ada became keenly aware that she still needed more income to do what she wanted to do. Specifically, she wanted to make sure she had no problem satisfying on time all her fixed expenses. And, she wanted a telephone like her neighbor had. Her first venture to accomplish this was to try a domestic employment job. Her first house-cleaning job was for a young Anglo single mother who lived in a small duplex about five miles from her home. She took Wee Wee with her. Arriving and going into the young ladies home, she was surprised at how small the place was and even more appalled at the condition inside. It did not compare at all to her own house and its space. Ada's decision to resign immediately was prompted by Wee Wee's simple question when they got home—"Mama you're not going back there are you?" Ada's simple reply was that she would have to think about it. But she knew that very moment she would not be returning.

Lying in bed that night she thought about how they had rented the home place in Rockdale, and why couldn't she do the same here by increasing the size of the house? And since there was a deep back yard, she could add more but separate rooms. As a community of active military residents as a result of the war stationed at the military bases in the San Antonio Area, young Negro men at Fort Sam Houston Base who were not eligible for housing on the base needed housing facilities for their families. She felt she could do something about that, but she needed resources to do it.

Having heard of a place called Betty's Eat Shop on Commerce Street a mile form home, she decided to bake her special lemon meringue pie and Apple lattice pie and try her sales skill by taking them to the restaurant. Rufus Waiters, her next door neighbor who had a car drove her to the restaurant.

The proprietor laughed at her proposition. Ada looked around at the packed place with uniformed soldiers. And she thought, this has to work as she heard Rufus Waiters say, "Sir, I guarantee you wont laugh after eating a piece of either one of her pies. And you can test it on some of your customers as a sample test."

The test went over more than expected and there was request after request for additional pieces. The proprietor was astonished and realized he did not want this golden calf to disappear because if she could cook pies like that she was capable of cooking other things. Going back into Betty's office he spoke about this 'gold mine' discovery and that she needed to hire her. Saving a piece of both pies for her, he encouraged her to taste either one. She did and immediately told him to hire her.

In due time Ada had amassed enough funds to start her building project plan. She hired her cousin Eric Joiner who was a painter at Kelly AFB, but who could do any kind of construction work. She had witnessed what he had done on his own home without the use of any licensed contractors or skilled workers. Most family and friends thought him to be an illiterate. His language skills lacked anything close to the formal English language, but Ada recognized his God-given talents and skills. His skills included carpentry, plumbing and electrical work without error.

Ada's first undertaking was an additional room on the back of the main house. A 50-year-old single woman named Flossie was an immediate first tenant for the new room. She had the privilege to use the bath room facility inside.

Subsequently Ada ventured into build a three-room apartment and a one-room stucco building directly behind the apartment building.

And she had a closet built on the back of the main house that housed a commode for the apartment and single room building tenants to use. She still had room for the building of a storeroom that housed her washing machine with rollers attached. There was still space for her garden and chicken coop enabling her grocery store purchases affordable.

Tenant flow was continuous as the military deployment of some service men occurred, others came as they got the word of this generous landlord who lived not far from the entrance gate to the Fort Sam Houston Army Base. All who lived at Ada's dwelling were treated as though they were family. They occasionally sat at her dinner table. She became a sounding board for those who were troubled at times or had personal issues.

CHAPTER 36

A Terrifying Experience

Having gone through her loss of her soul mate and best friend, her beloved husband Ike, the year 1942 was almost a replica of the Death Angels visit to Ada's family members. Four thirty a.m. February 19, 1942 Onie her youngest brother in Fort Worth, Texas was shot and killed. A couple of months later her youngest sister Fannie passed in Lubbock, Texas. She was in her mid twenties. She and her husband Gus the anglo looking bootlegger and proprietor of a dozen cottages for the purpose of business of unlawful activity of the overnight college dwellers.

Gus and Fannie had no children, but Fannie loved Ada's little girl. Each year she sent her a toy at Christmas time. The most cherished of which was the beautiful Shirley Temple Doll with the curly locks.

Gus informed Ada that Fannie's body would be shipped to Lexington, her funeral and burial would be there. He wanted Ada to travel with him back to Lubbock to make a decision about the disposition of Fannie's belongings.

The funeral was a somber one because of the anger each family member felt about this untimely death. The family buzz was that Fannie's death cause fostered suspension. All of the siblings felt that someone had killed their youngest family member.

Traveling to Lubbock, Texas with Gus and his brother Magnus who chose to drive because he felt compassion for his brother. He felt Gus was mentally stressed with all that had occurred—the funeral arrangements, the funeral, the travel, and the convicting eyes of the Lexington locals who knew the Green family and had watched Fannie from birth to her departure and marriage to Gus.

Ada was overwhelmed with the travel. This was the farthest she had traveled in her lifetime. And so the mountainous scenery was fascinating to her and why she stayed awake while all others in the car were sleeping. During this beautiful vision of nature, Ada realized that the car was heading toward the mountain edge and she screamed "Magnus." Fortunately Magnus, who had fallen asleep himself, turned the steering wheel to the right instead of the left that prevented the car from going over the mountain edge and perhaps the death of all inside had the car plunged over the edge and landed at the base of the mountain. Ada's awareness saved all of them this possible fate.

At Gus' home, Ada spent a day assisting Gus in boxing all of Fannie's clothes and some personal items. She directed Gus to mail the prepared boxes to Mollie who lived in Lexington. The idea was that Mollie could make distribution of all of the clothing to their nieces in the Lexington countryside.

Getting back to San Antonio, Ada prayed in a posture of adoration, praise and thanksgiving to the almighty God she served for his grace and mercy manifested through his traveling sustaining grace and protection for her and her little girl in the longest travel she had experienced in her lifetime. And she and her daughter were home to testify about the blessings they had received.

For a few months things seemed to be considered normal family activities. But October of this seemingly infamous year, Ada found herself traveling back to Lexington for the family matriarch Isabel—her mother—had died Sunday October 18, 1942 at 10:00 a.m. Isabel was 75 years old. She was a diabetic who had not been privileged to receive appropriate treatment, and not realizing the consequences without the treatment needed. Many felt, however, her death was the result of her grief of her two youngest children's death. All of Ada's siblings still among the living and all of the cousins assembled in the little church in Lexington for Isabel's celebration of life ceremony. There was not a dry eye among those attending. Isabel had been the perfect wife, mother and neighbor, and so, the entire community including the local merchants were touched by this one spirit, her persona and her lifestyle—specifically how she functioned as a widow and head of household.

Traveling back to San Antonio and home, Ada prayed for composure for the tears just wouldn't stop. She wanted her daughter to see her strength not her weakness. But, her discerning little daughter said, "Mama, I know how you feel. Just cry as long as you need to. Because if this happened to you, I know I couldn't stop." Ada had to laugh inwardly at this sage remark. It did give her some slight control of her emotions during the remaining travel home.

Wee Wee helped when she started talking about this great object Mrs. Blount had in her house that she discovered when she was sent to Mrs. Blount to tell her about their departure. Ada was curious and urged the child to tell her about her discovery. With a great deal of excitement Wee Wee told about this black electrical device that sat on a table they called a telephone. She talked about how they could talk to somebody in another house even in another city. Mrs. Blount allowed her to pick up the phone when it rang and say "Hello." And she heard through this strange piece of equipment at her ear someone say, "Hello! Is Mrs. Blount in?" She was so overwhelmed by what she heard, she became for the first time in her life mute. And she handed the phone to Mrs. Blount who commenced having a conversation with a person in another house.

In the Negro community, those having phones had a rather strange contractual agreement. They had what was called a "Party Line" which meant that they did not have total privacy. Others were on the same line which meant one could actually listen to another users conversation as they talked. Each of the users had the same privilege.

After Ada's visit with Mrs. Blount, Ada knew she had to have one, and she convinced her cousins in San Antonio to get one. And she sent letters to her siblings in Lexington, Cameron and Temple, Texas explaining how important this instrument was.

Despite Ada's family loses, she knew she had a responsibility to nurture and raise a child who was fast moving toward adulthood. She prayed constantly that God would allow her to live to see her daughter become an educated Christian young woman. Her daily efforts centered on this mission.

CHAPTER 37

Health and Strength Need

Ada being cognizant of the fact she needed to stay healthy for her child's sake and her own, she did everything she knew how to maintain good health for herself and her child. For whatever reason or medical authority Cod Liver Oil Pills were a main medical product in her medicine cabinet, and her little girl was given one to swallow every day. Ada knew she had much on her plate as head of household. One thing her little girl now twelve years old, a ninth grader, was graduating from the Holy Redeemer Grammar School. More importantly, she was the valedictorian of her class.

The graduating ceremony was a joyous event for the family and neighborhood friends who attended to watch this tiny little girl with given name of Dolores Maxine Woods (AKA Wee Wee). She was the smallest of the graduates to walk to the middle of the stage and give a dynamic speech citing in part her growth and development in designing and sewing clothes. Comically she mentioned about the gaiety of the bazaars held and the making of the delicious caramel vanilla candy bars the sisters made from their donations of sugar and canned evaporated milk. A roar and hand clapping from the audience followed this declaration. The rest of her speech featured endeavors of the class to complete high school and continue to higher education and what could be the result of their efforts. This tiny little girl got a standing ovation from the audience. Even her classmate Israel Cunningham, her runner-up, who rendered the salutatorian speech was impressed and gave her a resounding hand clap.

CHAPTER 38

The Education Decision

High school selection for Ada's young very vulnerable daughter was an issue. She had two choices—Phyllis Wheatley the only Negro public high school in this booming Texas city of San Antonio. Separate but equal was the philosophy for the operation of state public schools or the Saint Peter Claver Academy. This was a Parochial school that required tuition from students who attended. Either choice required the child to take two buses to get to school. If she attended Wheatley High school, she would have to take the S. P. Depot Bus four blocks from her home at New Braunfels Ave. and Commerce streets and transfer downtown. Then she had to walk four blocks to Houston street to board the Wheatley special bus that transported Negro children from the west side of town and the east side to the school located on Gabriel Street east of New Braunfels Ave. School integration was a thing of the far future. If she chose the Parochial school, her daughter would still have to take the S. P. Depot Bus downtown but transfer to the regular city Nolan Street Bus that stopped directly across from the school at the corner of Liveoak and Nolan Streets. Ada wanted her little girl to continue in a catholic school because of its Christian foundation that on a daily basis taught Christian doctrines and values through its catechism course.

So September 1943 Ada's little 13 year old daughter Dolores Maxine Woods enrolled in the catholic school. Dolores AKA Wee Wee still maintained the status of being the smallest in her class. She adjusted quite well, was liked by all of her teachers who recognized her potential. One hurdle she had to cross was the attitude of mother superior the principal. Her verbal attack on this tiny girl was in the basement science class. She accused her of being a deserter from the Catholic Church. The young girl was stunned by the sister's statement. For her parents were responsible for her leaving the Catholic Church.

Like a very old citizen Dolores felt the need to set the matter strait. She got up from her seat, went to Mother Superior's desk and asked if she could go and talk to her in her office after school. Reluctantly Mother Superior gave her permission, and that was probably because she saw the determination in this tiny student's demeanor having the boldness she had to even request a meeting. The meeting was held, however, in the basement that had a dungeon like atmosphere. The little girl's heart began to have a heavy thump, and she began speaking with some apprehension about what the Mother Superior's action would be. But, she had learned in her spiritual growth that one needed to tell the truth no matter the circumstance because God was listening. Looking, with her big brown eyes, straight in the face of Mother Superior she began her explanation emphasizing the fact that it was her parents' decision not hers. But, she felt they were justified in what they did because their next door neighbors—the Waiters—niece Theresa a student and graduate of Holy Redeemer school had been groomed for and was sent to Louisiana to become a nun. She went on to say that her father, who was a great man, passed away when she was ten, that she was an only child. Her mother and father could not think of loosing another child as they had lost a son at birth ten years before she was born. She ended her diatribe with, "That's what I know about it. They couldn't see me becoming a nun and living in another place." Mother Superior had a hard time maintaining her composure certainly desiring to laugh at the sincerity to this tiny little girl who seemed to be much stronger than her physical appearance. Mother Superior took a step forward towards Dolores. And the child didn't know whether to step back or run. But, her adrenaline caused her to freeze. Surprisingly, the top nun tapped her on the shoulder and with a half smile told her to "get to class."

Apparently there was a discussion about this little girl with nuns who were her teachers at the dinner meal. It was determined based on her performance in the classes that she was bright, an achiever, and some might brand an exceptional student. If the child had been a fly on the wall she would have heard the Mother Superior instruct her teachers to challenge her because this one was worthy to be a "keeper."

The next week Wee Wee received a lot of attention from the teachers. She was taking Spanish, but the French teacher wanted her to take French during her study hall period. The music teacher invited her to take violin classes and the after school lay dance teacher Mrs. Mattie Terrell. She was her aunt Agnes next door neighbor, who had taught her and her cousin Agnes Ellen (AKA Nupie) to do the 'Loop-T-Loo' when they were five years old. She was thrilled at this and became a member of Mrs. Terrell's 'Terpsichorean Dance Group.' The Violin venture after a few days was determined a 'no, no.' Students in the class had been in this art form since they were practically in diapers so she thought and certainly proficient in their ability and executions. Wee Wee having gone to the third grade in piano music with several qualified instructors let her mother know she should not be wasting any more money in this music study. She also opted out of taking French during her study period. Her reasoning was that she did not want to fail in any subject, and she had enough on her education acquisition plate to prepare her for college.

Dolores (AKA Wee Wee) made friends easily with other high-end-achieving students and she had a close friend Jimmie Joyce Morrison who had come from Holy Redeemer with her. They had two things in common. They were reared by a widowed and single mom.

Dolores liked particularly the dances at two o'clock in the afternoon in the gym just about every other day. She had a special partner who was an excellent dancer—Alvoyd Wilson. The boy could cut a rug. The climax of this young thirteen-year old high school sophomore's year was being asked and going to the prom. Ada made her a beautiful organza royal blue formal gown. Sonny Lewis her escort, another thirteen year old drove up in a car that had the appearance, because of its length, of a hearse. He presented her with a royal blue dyed carnation corsage that matched her dress. Ada struggled to protect her fear, but mustered up to tell the young Sonny Lewis to have her back by nine o'clock that evening. His reply was, "Yes ma'am." Off they traveled to this grand affair.

Music for this prestigious affair was furnished by Mr. Abrams band composed of Phyllis Wheatley High School selected band students. And their goal was to play the most popular dance music of the day. And they did during the entire course of the evening.

Now it was a fact that Sonny was not a great teenage dancer of the time. But Alvoyd Wilson, Dolores' school dance partner, was there and she had the opportunity to be on the dance floor throughout the evening as she described to Ada when she returned home on time as specified by

Ada. Now Sonny didn't much mind all the dancing Dolores did because it kept him from being embarrassed with his 'two left feet.'

Ada watched her little daughter attract several suitors during her high school years at her school and from the public high school. And she had a different escort to the prom for each of the three years of her high school attendance. The 1944-1945 school year Kenneth Dominique was her escort. Kenneth was a very handsome teenage Creole. Were it not for his hair texture, he could have passed as a white boy. He was the son of the prominent Don Albert who owned the very popular Key Hole Night Club on the west side of town in the Negro community there. The 1945-1946 year, Wee Wee's senior year, her escort was Britton Armstead a popular young teenager from Wheatley High School. His popularity stemmed from the fact that he was a musician and was a member of Mr. Abrams' Wheatley High School band special group who had provided music for Saint Peter Claver Academy the previous year. He was not as tall as her previous escorts, and he had two left feet. He couldn't dance like the parochial school students. Their purely platonic girlfriend-boyfriend relationship lasted until their high school graduation and departure for college.

Being on the honor roll through her three years at the Academy was something for Ada to be proud of, but her tiny little daughter became an unsuspected entrepreneur. Each day this teenager would make a stack of delicious ham sandwiches—at least three. Now Ada never questioned her about the number of sandwiches. Well, Saint Peter Claver Academy was also a boarding school. And there were as many out-of-town, out-of-state students as there were locals. Boarders always had a yearning for something home cooked or prepared as a delicious ham sandwich, thus the need of the sandwich extreme Dolores prepared. She sold them to the boarders who requested every day. Now there was a personal purpose for this undertaking. She and her friend Jimmie Joyce loved the movies. Proceeds from this endeavor allowed her and Jimmie Joyce, who had her own resources, to travel after school downtown to the Original Mexican Restaurant on Losoya Street to purchase hot tamales to go. They could not eat in the restaurant because they were Negroes, and they didn't want to. They simply gathered their packages, walked back to the front of the school, crossed the street to travel down Liveoak to Commerce Street. Turning left on Commerce St. they had to pass some extremely shaky businesses. Those considered to be in this "red light district" of the population were the "Foggy Bottom" and the "Avalon Grill." But each Friday after school they did it bravely to get to the next block and the Cameo Theater—the Negro movie theatre. From her weekly sales, Dolores had enough money for the movie ticket and popcorn. She already had bus fare from Ada. Dolores and Jimmie Joyce always got out in time to get the eastbound S. P. Bus and get home on time.

Ada never felt the need to question her enterprising young daughter about the extra sandwiches she made on certain days. She knew her little girl was definitely not gaining any weight, and was still a very selective eater never going for seconds and never eating everything on her plate at mealtime.

Getting her daughter settled in a high school situation that seemed to be very comfortable to her, was another milestone accomplished in the 1941 year for Ada. She gained new friends who lived in the city and some who were boarders from other Texas towns—her real customers in her sandwich selling business.

As most young people look forward to that very special day when they will don a cap and gown for the prestigious ceremony called graduation, a bombshell was decreed by the city. This was made based on the city Health Department's indicating that the city was in what they believed to be an epidemic threat. The city issued an ordinance that there could not be any large assemblies of people especially like the graduation exercises. It was the time of the polio epidemic. But the Catholic nuns at this notable St. Peter Claver Academy property because of their very close contact with their creator through prayer decided on a strategy to circumvent the city Ordinance. The school had a courtyard in between the elementary school classrooms and the high school two-story with basement building. These buildings prevented the sight of the courtyard from the intersecting streets of Nolan and Liveoak. So these conscientious nuns had parish members who had construction and carpenter skills to build risers in the courtyard to accommodate the 50 graduates—16 boys and 34 girls who were decked out in white robes and caps. The brave graduates, standing on the risers, were flanked on both sides by two parish priests. The priests supported the ordinance breach. The celebration went off without a hitch, and the student graduates and their parents felt they were justified in their law-breaking venture.

Now higher education was Ada's plan for her daughter. Prairie View A & M College near Hempstead, Texas was the college choice because Patricia Jennings, Alene Jordan and Jimmie Joyce Morrison had been accepted at the college. Jimmie Joyce, Wee Wee's classmate throughout elementary and high school, was her roommate their freshman year.

Ada was a constant visitor to the college, and she was honored and happy to see not only Wee Wee's roommate but also her dorm friends. Their affection probably was based on the great food items Ada brought and mailed periodically were shared with them.

During her daughter's four years of college, Ada knew she was happy with her school choice and the friends she had acquired. Most profound was the fact that this petite teenager attracted several suitors. In fact having maintained her virginity she was engaged to a different one each year at the college. There the exceptional, smart poet Charles Donaldson who came to visit her the summer after her first year ended, and on a beautiful moonlit night down at Lamelle's park near the Salado Creek he placed a ring on her finger. But Charles one of the "Dukes"—a prestigious male group on the campus—did not return to the campus Wee Wee's sophomore year to complete his work. And a new romance occurred with Roland Martin a young veteran whose sister was on the college staff. Naturally he was older than the other pursuers. She returned Charles' ring but she did not accept Roland's ring because he too the following year did not return as a student. In comes the Studebaker car owner and oil man—Edgar Davis—a handsome Creole from Houston, Texas. He took her from the train station on her way home for the Christmas break and drove her to San Antonio. Also in the car were Dorothy Bright whose father lived in San Antonio and Carlos another Creole and male friend of Edgar.

He not only gave Wee Wee an engagement ring, but also the wedding band. This engagement fizzled out probably because on his second visit to San Antonio during summer vacation Wee Wee was shocked at his attempted date rape. But despite his physical build compared to hers she prevented it from happening. Maybe it didn't happen because he had real compassion for her. By all means she was not going to let happen to her what she knew had happened to her cousins who now had babies.

Wee Wee didn't hesitate to tell Ada what had happened. Ada laughed, and Wee Wee felt it was strange that her mother had that kind of reaction to this devastating experience she had. However, Ada introduced her to the douche bag.

Now this young adult who graduated from high school at age fifteen with high hopes of graduating from college at nineteen was very frugal in managing her resources. Each summer during her vacation period, her cousin Laura Bell was able to convince her boss at the Grayson's Department Store to hire her for the summer. And so, she was and held such lofty positions starting with operating the human mechanical electric elevator in the store, then to presser and lastly to stock room clerk. The money she earned, she used wisely. She would not buy tooth paste or deodorant considered absolute needed commodities. In lieu of these essential items she would purchase an Arm and Hammer box of soda. It was a perfect powder for brushing her teeth, and she made her deodorant with a portion of soda and enough water to make a paste. So on the campus she had the privilege of having resources to treat herself to the great bacon and egg sandwiches, and the great hamburger in the Wreck Hall where she was an avid table Tennis (ping-pong) player. She often cut class to do so. She was shrewd in this act in that she never cut class to the extent that she was called in and questioned about her actions by the dean nor a counselor. Another unusual trait of this young 18-year old was that the break up of her several fiances did not seem to affect her. Probably, this was because she never experienced the ultimate in a male-female intimate relationship. And so this final year of her college endeavors there were two suitors. Frisco, another handsome Creole from Houston, Texas was one. He could frequent the college campus often. During Wee Wee's travel through Houston to get home for the Christmas school break, Frisco's mother called Ada and asked permission for Wee Wee to stay over night while she was in Houston for her train connection. A big dance was being held in Houston that night and her son wanted to take Wee Wee to this special event. Surprisingly Ada consented. The two young people on the dance floor that night were dance spectaculars. Both were excellent dancers, and they made an excellent match on the dance floor. In fact they became a central attraction on the dance floor. That night after the dance to accommodate the sleeping factor in this two-bedroom home, Wee Wee slept with Frisco's mother and Frisco slept with his father. There was nothing that could occur between the two young superb dancers but exhaustion and sleep from their non-stop dancing at the dance. The second person in this triangle was the young divorcee Frank White III in San Antonio. He was a drop-out from Prairie View who happened to be at the train station bidding his cousins farewell as they were returning to P.V. and he was remaining in San Antonio. Wee Wee happened to be boarding this same train and making her first entrance to the P.V. campus. His cousin introduced him to Wee Wee. And that was the end of the situation so it seemed.

But, here in her senior year, Wee Wee meets this young man again at a party Sarah Ann Ziegler—her hairdresser—was having. A relationship sparked. Now this young man could not compare in looks and statue of the two former suitors and the current one in Houston. But, he was debonair and the leader of a pack of young men who acted as though he was their God. All were bigger and certainly more robust than he was. And they were all involved in the new trend of personal ecstasy—smoking marijuana. These young men would not, however, date girls who smoked this mind-affecting drug. The San Antonio suitor and the Houston suitor would never see each other so Wee Wee had no problem with being in the company of either.

Darkness still loomed during the end of what should have been the brightest days. During the first semester of her final year Wee Wee's practice-teaching assignment off campus was Bryant, Texas a small town that allowed the college to send potential teacher candidates to do their practice-teaching in their elementary and secondary schools. Wee Wee went to Kemp High School where she taught as an English major Spanish. Her high school background and college prowess in this discipline allowed her to succeed in this endeavor. And because she looked like the majority of the freshmen girls at the school, each morning she sprayed a gray streak in her hair so she could have that appearance of maturity.

CHAPTER 39

The Revenue Expansion

During her daughter's college years, ingress and egress of young service men and their families in her rentals was great financial gain for Ada. And her serving a luncheon meal for the Creole hotel owner Cuzan Lemelle, her seamstress endeavors of making garments and doing alterations kept her busy. In addition church activities involved serving as a very committed usher for morning and evening services. And even though she knew about Japan's attack on Pearl Harbor 12/7/1941 that caused the United States to enter the World War II Campaign that had begun in September 1, 1939, her conversations to her young tenants about the matter were brief. For always in her mind was where Ike would be with this conquest. And so with all of her endeavors and work, she was determined to have a great family Christmas gathering and a feast no one would forget. Not only were family members delighted with her kitchen prowess, but her tenants were overwhelmed at the culinary skills of this very giving petite lady. Not having a dining room table that would accommodate all the family and dinner guests, participants were eating in stations all over the house except the bathroom.

CHAPTER 40

The Unexpected Abduction

All seemed to be going quite well as Ada's daughter and another P.V. student shared a room at Mama Crenshaw's (affectionately called by former P.V. student tenants) home. But, returning from a visit home during a weekend by bus, Wee Wee arrived back in Bryant, Texas near midnight. And even though walking from the bus station to Mama Crenshaw's home would be an easy walk, it was pitch black dark with no significant street lights where she had to walk. Fearful of possible consequences, she chose to take the only Negro cab in Bryant believing this to be the best and safest action. It was not a good Idea. As she noted on the take off he was not driving in the direction to the house where she had been assigned to be a temporary boarder by the college practice teacher counselor. Instead he kept driving for several miles out of the city limits and drove into what appeared to be a continuous field of tall corn stalks. He stopped. This 18 year-old young adult was petrified. But, she reached back into her spiritual toolbox and began talking as she looked at this ball headed man sitting in the driver's seat. Having no knowledge of her thirty-minute diatribe, she stopped talking. Without a word this strange taxi driver who appeared to be middle aged cranked up the car. He did not say a word. He did not touch her, but drove back to town without stopping until he reached the Crenshaw home. The frightened young adult jumped out of the car ran into the house and never looked back, and neither did she pay the cab fare. And he didn't ask for it, but drove off hurriedly. Lesson learned, she would never get in a cab alone in Bryan, Texas.

The practicum ending in November, Wee Wee and her roommate returned to the P.V. Campus and readied themselves for the Christmas vacation departure.

Ada was extremely happy to see her little girl when she picked her up from the train station. Ross Mitchell her new next door neighbor who now occupied the Waiters's house on the eastside of her house provided Ada transportation to pick up her daughter. It was Ada's opportunity to introduce this kind and gentle but robust 275 pound, 6ft plus, dark skinned man whose eyes were not always focused normally. Yes, he was a second suitor for Ada, and Wee Wee sizing him up she couldn't see how her petite beautiful mother could choose him over Mr. Devane a debonair, handsome Creole widower from the westside of town. Wee Wee had never seen him in any way but "dressed up." He was always dressed in a three-piece suit and a provocative hat. As a result of his wife's death the year before he met her mother, he was so enamored with Ada that he presented her with many household items and personal things of his deceased wife. Ada really had no desire nor need for the fancy china and other expensive household items. But Ross, the next door neighbor, was gifted and talented with the ability to do any home repairs plumbing or electrical. It was soon discerned by Wee Wee that Ross was her choice and he was nice and helpful to her in her transition efforts to and from college.

During the 1941-1951 period Ada was the perfect landlord and mother figure for the continuous flow of young service men and their wives and children. And she was still the 'go to' member in her family.

It was during this period that Bertha (Betty) her oldest sister called and asked for help for her youngest daughter Louisa who was a few months younger than Wee Wee. Louisa had managed to contract a dreaded venereal disease, and Bertha knew she could not be helped in Lexington, and she had no faith in the surrounding small towns' provision for this problem. The young adult came to Ada. She was taken to a doctor, treated for her problem and stayed with Ada until she was declared cured. This being accepted by the physician, Louisa returned to her family in the Lexington countryside, went back to college and earned a degree.

CHAPTER 41

An Unforeseen Roadblock

Ada was so proud seeing her daughter off to school for her last semester and potential graduation. The head of fate steps in and three weeks after returning to school, this potential graduating senior took sick. She was having difficulty breathing. She didn't have a cold, cough or fever. The campus physicians were stumped and Ada was called to come and pick up her daughter immediately. She did with Mr. Mitchell her neighbor providing the transportation.

Ada knowing she had to do something quick, she thought about the healing physician everybody talked about in Seguin, Texas 34 miles away. With the services of Ross Mitchell again, she bundled her daughter up and traveled to Seguin. The doctor everyone talked favorably about was in his late 70's and had physical problems himself as one could see with the deterioration of his fingers which tips had been painted with a violet colored medication. He was in fact a philanthropist who served indigents without or very little when they came for service. He had a fluoroscope machine in which he could observe the internal structure of the body—x-ray device.

Realizing this was a young female college student and what could probably be the problem as he had encountered with others. Immediately he administered this x-ray test and seemed very happy to say, "Well there is no baby in there." Ada was startled at this remark and Wee Wee thinking without a doubt it would be another immaculate conception slightly laughing through her pain. After the doctor's complete examination of this young adult patient his diagnosis was that she had pleurisy and inflammation of the pleura that usually caused painful and difficult respiration, cough and expedition into the pleural cavity. She didn't have fever, which may have been the diagnostic problem of the P.V. doctors. This very frail Seguin doctor used a material to wrap her body tightly from directly under the breast to slightly above the stomach areas and he recommended bed rest until her breathing became normal.

This roadblock meant that this potential college graduate would not accomplish this at age nineteen as she had so desired.

Now Ada remembering the strict military pension directive realized she needed to inform the Veterans Administration of her daughter's physical status. With the help of her friend and confidant Gussie, she composed a letter and mailed it to the VA March 17, 1950. She received the following letter from the Veterans Administration:

VETERANS ADMINISTRATION
District Office No. 10
1114 Commerce Street
Dallas 2, Texas

APR 4, 1950
Your File Reference
Reply refer to DA8BA
XC 048089
WOODS, Isaac

Mrs. Ada Woods
2007 Wyoming St.
San Antonio, Texas
Dear Mrs. Woods:

Your award of death compensation or pension as unremarried widow of the above named veteran has been amended at the rates indicated below on account of school termination by the veteran's child, Dolores Maxine Woods

If this child resumes school complete attached 674 and return to this office

Monthly Payment	Commencing Date	Ending Date
$54.00	9-1-46	2-28-50
$42.00	3-1-50	

Your account will be adjusted as soon as possible.

IMPORTANT: The veterans Administration must be notified immediately of the death, marriage, or CHANGE OF ADDRESS of any person receiving death benefits. If at any time the income of a dependent parent is increased, notice thereof must be furnished. Prompt notice must also be furnished if a child over eighteen for whom benefits are being paid discontinues the approved course of instruction or enters upon another course of study.

Severe penalties involving fines and imprisonment are provided by the laws of the United States when a person fraudulently accepts any payment to which he is not entitled or obtains or receives money with intent to defraud the United States.

Very truly yours,
O. B. Freeman
Chief, Dependents

FL 8-99

Beneficiaries
Jul 1948 Claims Division

CHAPTER 42

Overcoming a Set Back

It didn't dampen Wee Wee's spirit that she became a dropout. No, she bounced back and was back on campus for a summer semester in which she needed one course that was not offered during the fall semester—Shakespeare. And she was determined to be a mid-term graduate in January 1951. This she accomplished but did not return to march at the ceremony.

Ada discerned her daughter's relief having crossed another milestone in her young life, and she could see her present interest was another significant life venture—marriage.

Ada had a concern about this new fiance Frank White III—the fourth. She and most observers felt he was truly the least of the previous three. Five feet seven, 135 pounds he didn't have the statue, the looks or the financial promise. But he had a charm that was enough to marry and divorce a preacher's daughter in Kerrville, Texas where his grandmother lived and where he stayed at times, and claimed to have been engaged to a nurse in San Antonio who still longed for him. He received Ada's favor on his first date with her daughter when he addressed her as "Mama Woods." He also had male followers that treated him as if he were their high priest. Each one could look down on him, pick him up and toss him if they had the inclination. They didn't. Dickey Wade, one of his followers, just wanted his wife-to-be.

CHAPTER 43

The Nuptials

The latter part of January wedding plans began. Ada was good at everything she did, but she was not a socialite. She was not aware of the usual protocol for such and event. Instead of a flowing white wedding gown, her daughter selected a beautiful but inappropriate white tailored fine textured suit. Instead of a white veil over her head and face, she donned a burnt orange hat with matching burnt orange spaghetti strap high heeled shoes.

The wedding scene was in Ada's living room. Frank's cousin May Dell Cherry provided the music, and Ada's pastor, Reverend B. Tyree Alexander, officiated. It was done. There was no real reception just a cake and punch for the small group participating. There was no honeymoon, and the two young newly weds were given an apartment status in Ada's house allowing them to make changes as they wished in the three rooms provided.

Monday following the wedding the groom reported to his work site at Kelly AFB. Dolores became the dotting wife with a vision of her own home with the white picket fence. Considering her own desire for employment, she realized there was only one Negro high school where she could teach and she felt someone would have to die before that happened. Not having attended public school in the city, she was not aware of the under-the-table money exchange with a certain Negro principal that could make her employment possible. So with her one year of typing in high school she took a civil service test, passed and was hired as a pay grade 2 (qualified for a pay grade 4) Distribution Clerk in Procurement.

Ada was truly proud of her daughter even knowing how badly she wanted and was qualified for a teaching job at all levels.

As Ada continued her entering and deployment of young service men and their wives and their continuation of communication with her by letter and telephone, truly one would think she was an adoptive parent of all those young servicemen, their wives and their children. Not only did she respond to letters received, but she treated them as if they were her family as she sent birthday gifts, Christmas gifts and condolences. One family whose 21-year old son had enlisted in the army was sent immediately into the war zone. Within a week he was killed in action. Ada truly felt the pain of her former tenants as they shared this tragedy with her.

CHAPTER 44

A Needed Newness

The early '50s Ada's life seemed to have reached a needed calm. She watched her daughter's commitment to her job, and she knew by the glow in her daughter's face and her weight gain that she was going to be a grandmother soon. She became, however, concerned and yes apprehensive about the activities of her son-in-law—Frank. A month before her grandchild was due her apprehension became a reality because her dapper young son-in-law had been arrested for possession of the marihuana drug that she knew nothing about. She also learned in his period of incarceration that her daughter had been the frugal one of the two. For each paycheck she received she saved a certain amount. In fact she had saved $300.00 by 1951. Frank had been a spender having saved nothing. Wee Wee shared with Ada that Frank's mother Deloris having the same name as her daughter but spelled differently asked her to use the $300.00 she had saved for the purpose of her ensuing doctor and hospital bills for the birth of her first child to bail him out. The mother-in-law in Kerrville, Texas vowed that she would return the money at the end of the month. Ada advised her daughter to take a leap of faith and provide the money for her husband's release from jail. It was done. He was released. Ada seeing her son-in-law in a new light silently questioned his maturity and understanding of his role as husband, provider and soon-to-be father. He was two years older than Wee Wee.

As a result of this event during the coming months Ada could sense that her daughter wanted to and felt it necessary to move into a house of her own, but it was impossible because of the reckless spending of her son-in-law.

The month of May 1951, Ada could see the weariness of her daughter in the last stage of her pregnancy. May 5, Wee Wee's labor pains started and she and Ada walked two blocks down Connelly Street to the newly established Good Samaritan Hospital. The hospital building was the former Corinth Baptist Church where Ada and her daughter were members.

Going through the normal examination for the birthing process, Wee Wee was told it was not time. Five days she traveled to the hospital and was told the same thing. But, the fifth day in so much pain she rebelled stating that she was not going back home and that they needed to do something about her pain.

Her physician, Dr. C. L. Melenyzer, told the staff to admit her and to provide as much comfort as they could.

The hospital had profound restrictions on visitation times. And Ada knew this. But, as enterprising as she was, she found a way to be in that hospital until her grandchild was born. She watched the workers and where they picked up things to do their jobs. She donned an apron, found a broom and proceeded to provide janitorial services on the three floors of the hospital assuming the role of volunteer domestic worker. The staff knew what she was doing, but they also gleaned the love and passion this woman had for her only child. So, they pretended she was one of them.

May the 10th, the Saturday before Mothers' Day, head nurse Starr started the birthing process because the doctor was not there and she knew it was time. She administered the saddle block (a spinal anesthetic used to deaden the pelvic area). Wee Wee gave birth to a tiny five-pound baby girl just as the doctor arrived. Nurse Starr virtually screamed out, "It's a dam little girl, and she's pissing all over me." There was laughter among the medical team observing. Wee Wee fell asleep, and Ada was so relieved that her daughter and granddaughter were fine. The baby was given the name Andrea Lynn White.

CHAPTER 45

The Calm, The Storm, The Rainbow

The next 14 years Ada's experiences can best be described as the sweet and the sour or the good and the bad. Her altruistic habits still defined her spirit. Again in 1955 she walked the halls of the Good Samaritan Hospital with a broom to be the second to greet her new 7 pound, 6 ounce grandson who was given the name of Frank White III. Mother and son were in perfect condition. As Ada held and looked at this new grandson, she knew he was destined to be somebody special.

Ada knew with the addition of another child that her daughter yearned for her own house with the picket fence. Before little Frank was two months old her daughter and her husband were able to move into a new duplex on Fargo Street located in a new Negro/African American sub-division call the Coliseum east of the MKT train tracks where virgin land existed for years. Now homes in the Coliseum, the Willow Park Addition and the duplex apartments were built providing all the way to the Salada Creek decent dwellings for the defined low to middle class Negroes.

Ada was truly concerned about her daughter's welfare for she had discerned the lack of maturity in her son-in-law and her suspicion of his infidelity. Her consolation was constant prayer on her daughter and grandchildren's behalf.

As her grandson ushered in four months of life, Ada received a call from her daughter asking if her next door neighbor Ross Mitchell could come and move her belongings and furniture to her house. She was leaving Frank for she had experienced "the straw that broke the camel's back." Her husband had gone on another weekend spree, and when she arrived home that night, opened the door and turned on the light switch there was no light.

Knowing that her husband, as usual, would not be returning until Sunday evening, she was able to pack and move everything to Ada's house. She used her storehouse to store the furniture she had for the two bedrooms, one bathroom, living and dining room in the tiny Fargo duplex apartment she had enjoyed. It, however, had become almost a brothel for Frank's buddies and their female pickups. She left a candle in the middle of the living room floor of the apartment when she left.

As Ada watched her son-in-law's begging for her daughter to return with promises she doubted he had the ability to keep. She remembered how Wee Wee had shared a strange but disturbing act of her son-in-law. After one of his weekend sprees he had rushed in the apartment demanding that she needed to come with him and go to Seguin, Texas where they had to get a penicillin shot. Wee Wee went, but she realized that her husband as a result of his promiscuity had infection of some kind of venereal disease. This knowledge weighed on her decision to keep her distance from him. She thought about how she or any future children could be affected by his sinful actions.

Ada realized the strength of her daughter who had already returned to work at Kelly AFB. Ada could see that reconciliation was not on her agenda. In fact in her grandson's fifth month of life, her daughter secured the service of a recommended Divorce Lawyer and filed for a divorce.

With a no-contest factor the $35.00 divorce was rendered with the stipulation that her husband was to pay $50.00 a month for child support. He paid one $50.00 and with his nomadic instincts fled to Los Angeles, California never to return to San Antonio to live and never supported his two children in any way.

Ironically Laura Bell, Ada's niece and Joe, Ike's nephew, had also dissolved their marriage, and she left her nice home on Center Street and moved in a duplex on Ambrosia Street walking distance from where Wee Wee's duplex apartment was.

This was baffling to Ada because she believed that Joe had the qualities that made him a loving and caring mate and stepfather for Laura Bell's daughter. This divorce did not change the affection and belief in her husband's nephew. Joe continued his weekly, almost daily, visits to Ada's house. On his way to work at Randolph AFB he would bring his sugar cane bucket to Ada to get whatever leftovers his "aunt Ada" had in her refrigerator to fill his bucket. He knew, although Ada was not a habitual consumer of mind-altering beverages as he was, he sensed that occasionally she liked to drink a Falstaff beer. So many evenings he came to chat with her he would bring her a six pack. He would sit and engage in a long conversation with this woman he had such an affinity for and a special kindred for her and her daughter who was his natural blood kin.

Ada was careful in what food she consumed because a trip to the doctor following her surgery before her husband passed she was told she had an enlarged heart and was prescribed a miniscule white pill she took daily. And she kept always in the refrigerator a bottle that contained a mixture of garlic and water. When she felt a need, she drank a small portion of this concoction a Rockdale sage and friend had advised her to do when she had a certain body feeling that was not normal.

Laura Bell was able to sustain herself in her new resident because she had caused a special place in the mind of Mr. Margenthaler her employer who recognized her potential. Perhaps because he was a Jew he had no inhibitions about promoting this young Negro woman to an office managerial position. And in her 40 year career in the Grayson Department Store she was granted the coveted position of bookkeeper who was trusted each day to take the day's receipts to the bank a three-block walking distance from the store. She never had a problem.

CHAPTER 46

An Unimaginable Future

Ada's daughter, now a divorcee, and her same age cousin Nupie would on Saturday evenings during the 1956 year, for a one-night pleasure, take in the various upscale Negro nightclubs. Single young Negro men also gathered in these clubs. They danced and drank Coka Cola sodas. And the inevitable happened. Wee Wee met a dapper good looking 5'10" Creole looking guy who was serving as a part-time bouncer at the Spriggsdale Night Club. Wee Wee told Ada that she thought he was interested in Nupie, but she found out later that he was talking to Nupie to get her telephone number. She was his interest not Nupie.

And the courtship began with Rufus Lott a 42 year old clean-cut gentlemen who was divorced and had three children—two boys and one girl. His ex-wife had left the three children on the doorstep of his mother's home and returned to her Fairfield, Texas hometown. She returned only one time during the developmental stages of the children.

Ada was pleased with her daughter's relationship with this young man who was 16 years her daughter's senior. He had family members in the next block east of Ada's house. And considering the size and care of the homes of his uncle Ishman and his aunt Velma they probably could have been considered affluent Negroes. The uncle who was the spitting image of Rufus occupied one of the largest dwellings on the street and had a two-story rental over a two-car garage in their huge back yard. He had no biological children, but an adopted daughter named Adele. His aunt, whose resident was big also, had a son and a daughter. Ada learned that Rufus and this uncle had the similarity of a father-son relationship. For this reason and the maturity she observed in this potential son-in-law who had the capacity to render "dry wit" jokes that had most of his acquaintances declaring him a natural comedian. Ada was pleased with his candor as well as his attitude. But, he was a Methodist in good standing at the Jacob's Chapel United Methodist Church in sight and just a stone throw away across the street east of her home so he never thought of a comedic plunge.

Ada became the perfect baby sitter for her two-year old granddaughter and two-month old grandson when the great courtship began. She found it very difficult to keep from laughing as Wee Wee shared with her with great delight where they went on their special dates. The dog and rabbit chase sport in the deep country area was something Rufus and his friends took great delight in—even the betting process. And there was the great Runge, Texas reunion where descendents of the 52 Negro families assembled each year to celebrate. One, and only Hollywood, California celebrity, who came each year was a descendent of one of the families gained her celebrity status because she worked for the famous pianist Liboracie and was a great contributor for this cause. The chronicler for the event and the comprehensive document reflecting the names of the 52 original Runge Negro settlers and the descendents of each to date was Reverend Smith.

Now Ada had a feeling that it wouldn't be too long before wedding bells would ring. But she was totally surprised the way it happened. July 25, 1956 as she baby sat little Frank and Andrea Lynn allowing her daughter an opportunity to go and participate in a bridge luncheon hosted by Mavis Whitson Wee Wee's college friend. Mavis was married to Frank Whitson another college friend and they lived on Marmok street in the eastside Willow Park Addition. Before the games concluded, Rufus stopped by, picked up Wee Wee and drove to Seguin, Texas the small town 30 miles east of San Antonio. The two got a blood test, went before the Justice of the Peace and were married. Wee Wee dressed in a self-designed and made pink and white gingham dress was certainly not the attire of an imminent bride. Whatever was considered normal for this important event didn't happen. They were married and they had the papers to show for it.

Ada surprised, but relieved, embraced her new son-in-law offering her house and anything they needed that she could help them with.

Rufus had a small house on 'F' Street which he had put up for sale and had a potential buyer. He told Ada he wanted to dissolve all factors of his failed marriage and he felt it was an appropriate time to announce the fact that he would have custodial guardianship of his three children.

Ada discerned the progressiveness of her new son-in-law who was also employed at the Kelly AFB Motorpool. He had the privilege and pleasure to transport military brass and high-ranking politicians to various places in the city.

Although Ada made her home available to them, she had heard them privately talking about a new showcase house on Morningview Drive. It had been built, among others, in this Black Community by a Jewish developer named Golsby. The house was directly across the street from Rufus' younger brother Eldredge. Their problem was a down payment of $2,000.00. Neither had that much cash to spare. Hearing this Ada came to their rescue offering her help.

Now Ada rented her house from the elderly Sam Jacob, his daughter Anna Bell and her husband Dan Levin. This was a Jewish family who owned a commercial building at the corner of Commerce and New Braunfels and numerous rent houses in this community. Ada had the desire to buy the house she was renting. The elderly Sam Jacobs told her she would never pay for it. To Ada this was pretty much like the challenge she and her sister Mollie had in their childhood confrontation. It was a dare to her, and she was most determined to have it happen.

November 1950 she made a $515.90 down payment on a $2,200.00 note. She was to pay monthly installments of $20.00 or more each month that included interest at the rate of 6% per annum. Much to the chagrin of the Jacob and Levin family prediction, Ada now, by the grace of God, and as a Negro Femme Sole September 19, 1951 had paid for and owned her home.

Ada knowing that she had the collateral that could help the newly weds, she offered it. Rufus was extremely grateful and vowed he would pay off this loan in which Ada's house was used as collateral. She was able to secure a promissory note for the principal sum of $1,960.00 May 15, 1956 from Chris Andrade, Et Ux. She loved her daughter enough and trusted her son-in-law Rufus to put her home in jeopardy.

She knew how committed her daughter was in business matters coupled with the fact that she and her husband were gainfully employed at Kelly AFB.

Little did Ada know how her daughter's marriage to Rufus would impact her desire to become a teacher. A new elementary-junior high school had been erected on Nebraska Street near the Salada Creek just a 3-minute drive east from the couple's home. By divine providence the principal assigned to this new school was Virgil Walker her husband's first cousin. Ada's new son-in-law did not even know his new wife had a college degree and was certified to teach at all levels. Wee Wee shared that information with him. He was so excited about this discovery that he went to his brother's family across the street, his mother and sister up the street on Prelude and the principal's twin brother—Vernon—across the street in the 100 block of Morningview to share this breaking news. Within the week he took Wee Wee to the countryside where he was told his cousin, the principal was giving attention to his farmland. He was not disturbed by their visit according to Wee Wee's account to Ada, but was cordial, and impressed with the unusual interview and the applicant. So much so was he impressed that he hired her. He did not have available a teaching position, but he hired her for a dual position—Librarian and Counselor. This position included being textbook clerk, audio-visual coordinator and secretary for both disciplines. She had only 6 hours in Library Science as industry (elective) in her undergraduate work. The principal assured her that was okay. He had a former employee and friend—Mrs. Dorothy Pickett—who had experienced the same situation. She would be more than happy to help her to get started. And he advised her as Mrs. Pickett had done to get involved in acquiring certification in the two areas from Our Lady of the Lake College.

CHAPTER 47

The Grand Maternal Cultural Change

In the next decade of Ada's life she became the dotting grandmother and dedicated babysitter of an additional grandson—Rufus Jr. born March 15, 1958.

Ada was proud of her daughter during this period. In the eyes of Ada not only was she an exemplary wife, mother and stepmother, she was a perpetual student at Our Lady of the Lake College. During this period she worked fulltime. In addition, she was somewhat an ad hoc secretary for the Greater Corinth Baptist Church and Pastor B. Tyree Alexander. He would call on her to do special important correspondence for him, and she did the church bulletin. Unbelievably she also sold Avon Products. Ada never told her daughter she needed to slow down, but she would come to her home clean, cook and could be described as the built-in nanny for the pre-school grandson. She would even take the bus to Wee Wee's home and back to her house to save her and husband the driving. She was never late getting to Wee Wee's home to do her tasks.

Ada never pressured or asked about the important lien on her house. She trusted her son-in-law and daughter to make the necessary payments on time. June 10, 1960 she received the release of lien from Chris Andrade, Et Ux that was filed for record June 6, 1960. She was prayerful—thanking God for his blessings in the matter and the trustworthiness of her son-in-law.

CHAPTER 48

Political Interest

Although Ada was by no means a political "junky," but she was privileged to hear much talk about change occurring in America called the land of the free—specifically culturally. Was this anticipated change to elevate the Negro populace specifically in the south from second class citizenry to first class?

When she and her friend Julia Eato would attend meetings at the Fred Brock Post a great deal of talk went on about how and why change was occurring. Specifically they talked about the impact of: 1) the May 17, 1954 Supreme Court ruling unanimously in "Brown vs. Board of Education that racial segregation in public schools was unconstitutional, 2) December 1955 the refusal of Mrs. Rosa Parks to relinquish her bus seat to a white man was arrested, 3) how President Eisenhower federalized the Arkansas National Guard to escort 9 black students to an all white high school in Little rock Arkansas, 4) a rising star in the pulpit and the political agenda through a non-violent action to accomplish the equality of mankind black and white. This young Reverend Martin Luther King Jr. was founder of the Southern Christian Leadership Conference. He was elected the president of the organization. His ideology for righting the racial divide in this country was through a non-violent approach as he and his wife had spent a month in India studying Gandhi, and following the assassination of the N.A.A.C.P. President Medgar Evers in his home in Jackson, Mississippi, the young preacher and his organization strategically put into action August 28, 1963 the March on Washington. This was the first large integrated protest held in Washington D.C. And it was the place that King delivered his immortal "I have a Dream" speech.

Ada was so impressed with knowledge of the political changes voiced by the people who attended these meetings she became a member of the American Legion Post auxiliary #828, Fred Brock Unit on Nebraska Street.

As Ada and Julia attended these meetings often they were able to discern changes occurring in San Antonio. They no longer had to sit in the back of the bus or the balcony of the Majestic Theatre. Restaurants gradually saw the benefit of the Negro patron. Inner-city public and parochial schools became desegregated.

The first efforts in integrating faculties as Wee Wee shared with Ada was the transfer of fair complexioned Negroes (now referred to as African Americans) to the previous all-white faculty schools. They laughed and chuckled about it and called it "the peaceful" transition.

Shopping at Joske's Department store at the corner of Commerce and Alamo Streets downtown was a more pleasurable venture these days because they had the opportunity to have lunch in the beautiful "Camelia" restaurant in the basement of the store. They understood that much of the change that was occurring swiftly could also be attributed to the persistent efforts of the local civil rights activists.

At the Post speakers also expressed hope and confidence in a young man named John F. Kennedy who was the first Catholic and youngest president of the United States. He became a household conversation in Ada's home and the Negro community. This hope was crushed the sunny day of November 22, 1963 when he was assassinated by the racist Lee Harvey Oswald in Dallas, Texas as reported on the news and subsequent newspapers.

CHAPTER 49

The Magical Instrument

Being convinced by her daughter, Ada purchased a black and white television set that glorious instrument that changed many from radio listeners to TV viewers. Ada marveled at the fact that she could see human action in the form of news, variety shows and even movies. She thought it to be a phenomenal invention of man. She no longer had to listen radio drama such as Stella Dallas, Portia Faces Life, The Inner Sanctum and the movie station that presented Lux Presents Hollywood on Sunday evenings. This new gadget was what she needed for her past-time activity at home.

During this period Ada had an unexpected family shock. Her sister Ollie, Laura Bell's mother, came to San Antonio and Ada's home seeking medical help. Ollie a stately looking woman looked the picture of health, but she couldn't swallow water and definitely could not eat solid food. Ada immediately took her to Dr. Melenyzer her miracle doctor. But his diagnosis was grim to say the least. Ollie had cancer of the esophagus and had been treated by her doctor for bronchitis. The doctor advised that she go to a special cancer treatment hospital in Galveston, Texas. She went, but the voyage was in vain. A cure was impossible, and she expired the third day of her treatment. This was another gloom and doom experience for Ada as she realized the dwindling of her family of eleven siblings. Ollie's last rites, as was her younger sister, was held in Lexington, Texas. Although the remaining family members mourned her passing, they were not surprised because of Ollie's life style choices in Temple, Texas. She had no active relationship with her daughter Laura Bell or her only grandchild Laura Louise.

CHAPTER 50

Three

And then there were three—Bertha, Ada and Mollie. In the course of this time, Ada's siblings—Cissie, Della, Fate and Minor—crossed over Jordan as Ada described it, and "went to be with the Lord contingent on their individual salvation." All had young adult children except Cissie and Fate. As the Psalmist says "Weeping may endure for a night but joy comes in the morning," Ada experiences this joy as positive things were happening to her and her family.

To her surprise Ike's nephew Joe Lewis who had become so attached to Ada despite his failed marriage with her niece Laura Bell, brought to her a document February 18, 1960 that read: Designation of Beneficiary—Civil Service Retirement System. He made Ada the beneficiary of his $10,000.00 death benefit. She was overwhelmed knowing that she was only his aunt by marriage.

Her daughter, the love of her life, had successfully earned a Masters of Education Degree from the now Our Lady of the Lake University gaining certifications in Library Science, Counseling and Administration. While she was attending night classes to accomplish her goals and while achieving those goals she was still wife and mother as she provided her husband with two additional sons and Ada with her two additional grandsons—Vernon Keith born April 15, 1962 and David Terrence born February 13, 1964. Ada, in full support of her daughter's achieving her goals, felt she needed to help her by traveling with her and the two youngest children to the University for her night classes. There she sat and walked and did things to keep the two young energetic grandsons busy for the three hours—the time period of her daughter's classes. Ada was extremely proud when she found out that Wee Wee had been invited and employed to be a lecturer for an OLLU summer school course in Counseling.

Somehow Ada, observing her daughter's quest for continuing higher education, began to think of her desire to continue her education. She thought about her missed opportunity for a scholarship she had when she graduated from high school. She did not inform any family member of her desire, but enrolled and completed a course of study in The AKA College Department of Texas. She received a diploma that read in part:

THIS CERTIFIES THAT

Ada Woods

Has satisfactorily completed the Course of Study
And is found worthy of graduation and is hereby
Awarded this
Diploma
Given this 15 day of June in the year of our Lord
One thousand nine hundred and sixty At Austin,
Texas

Mrs. H.N. Lyle   Mrs. B.J. George
Department Secretary   Department President

No one dared to ask Ada what the course was about. She just received congratulations and hugs from all the family there.

Another blessing came from being advised by her friends Mollie and Mandrew Mitchell to file for Social Security. She did, and April 10, 1967 from the Department of Health, Education and Welfare Social Security Administration from the Kansas City, Mo. Payment Center she received a certificate of Social Insurance Award that reflected a monthly benefit of $35.00. She had already received 6/8/66 a notice of Health Insurance entitlement from the same department. The hospital insurance coverage under Title XVIII of the Social Security Act began July 1966. The medical insurance from the same source began July 1968. By virtue of the change in benefit rates due to "recent" amendments to the Social Security Act her monthly benefit increased October 1967 to $44.00 a month and February 1968 increased to $55.00. Her first check was in the amount of $341.00. She was delighted to say the least because when she applied for Social Security benefits June 1966 she was denied because she had not attained six calendar quarters of work. She had only five. To gain the one-quarter she needed, she started working part-time at the Ritz Motel—an African-American owned motel on East Commerce Street. Her new, somewhat disabled, tenant Nathaniel Bright was the head cook there. He had such an unprecedented adoration for Ada he convinced his boss that he needed more help in the kitchen and he had the perfect person for the job. Ada was hired.

Nathaniel was a Hempstead, Texas Creole cripple who migrated to San Antonio to live. Nathaniel's right leg was shorter than his left leg, and he had to wear a shoe with a built up sole and heel to relieve some stress in his walking. He would do anything for the affection of Ada, but Ada just did not see him in that manner. He would, however, do anything she asked or commanded of him. He took her fishing because he knew she loved to fish. And when she returned home whatever she had caught was fried and became a part of her dinner meal. And he took her on several trips to Lexington, Texas and its countryside to see Mollie and her ailing oldest sister Bertha called Betty by all who knew her. She prepared pots of cooked vegetables, roast and chicken to take to Betty because she felt she was not eating the proper foods for her health problem. Nathaniel was a miniscule replacement for Ross Mitchell—the big man—and the one Ada cast her affections on. Ross had moved from the house next door, and so he was no longer a daily presence in her life. Occasionally he would come back have lunch or dinner with her. Eventually the flame that once was between them became a "flicker" to finally go out.

CHAPTER 51

A New Emphasis

Church, her daughter's welfare, her grandchildren and her tenants became Ada's focus. Bertha's son Wilber, having completed his military tour of duty, and his wife Zedebee became her tenants as did Mrs. Blount's grandaughter Artemiese "Scobbie" and her husband Sam.

It was barely a day that passed that Ada did not receive a letter, a birthday card, Christmas greeting and mothers day card from former tenants who were now out of state residents. Not only did she answer every letter, she sent gifts to them and their children for Christmas, birthdays and high school graduation.

One of her special pen pals who had not been a tenant was Dorothy Swope, Nathaniel Bright's daughter who had been a college friend of her daughter. It was unfortunate that she had not been a part of her father's life though she loved him. She lived with and was nurtured by an aunt in Hempstead, Texas.

With her massive daily activities Ada never wavered in her church ministry serving on Usher Board #1 and participating in the activities of the Ladies Aide Society. And she became an avid viewer of the news on TV in the evening. She was devastated April 4, 1968 when she watched the broadcast on the assassination of Martin Luther King Jr. in Memphis, Tennessee the day after his immortal "I've Been to the Mountain Top" speech had been given. The thought that he was only 39 years old brought a continuous flow of tears. She pictured something like this happening to her child during this city's inner-city school desegregation enforcement. But, there was an even more close-to-home tragedy that had an effect on Ada's stress. Two very fine Christian women—a mother and her daughter—Mrs. C. M. Blanks, an active member of her church and her daughter Mrs. Victoria Dixon who was an active member of St. Paul United Methodist Church had been shot and killed. Mrs. Dixon's husband was the killer. This was an unprecedented, devastating tragedy that happened in the eastside Negro community December 31, 1968. It brought to Ada's mind her own son-in-law Rufus who was known to be quick to anger, act upon that anger and he was extremely jealous. But she had seen his love and devotion to her daughter and their children but had some reservation about his treatment of her grandson Frank. But she thought that perhaps he needed a strong male image that could help to deter his adopting his biological father's activity of a lawless nature specifically drug activities. Momentarily her thoughts came back to the current circumstances of the tragically murdered women and immediately thought of preparing food for Mrs. Blank's husband, her daughter Maceo and Mrs. Dixon's sons Paul and Russell.

CHAPTER 52

Effects of Stress

Now Ada the mother, grandmother, aunt, grandaunt and perpetual provider once again became the person everybody needed. Her home could very well have been described as Ada's Day Care Center. In addition to caring for pre-school grandson, Laura Bell's daughter Laura Louise who had married an army veteran sergeant years older than she also needed her service. Prior to this marriage she had an unsuccessful pregnancy and lost the child. As a result she was unable to get pregnant again. As she watched her cousin continue having children, she became obsessed with the idea of adoption. To make life a little easier in their home, her husband Tracy consented to the adoption frenzy. They adopted two beautiful little girls they named Sandy and Donna. Because Laura Louise worked as a clerk in a middle school and the central office the two little girls compatible in age with Wee Wee's two younger sons were placed in Ada's full day care.

Ada was a little concerned about how her new tenant Vincent White who was one of Mobile, Alabama civil service transfers to San Antonio would feel about this additional child-care service. He occupied the front east bedroom of the house where he certainly would be affected by the activities of the very active toddlers in Ada's living portion of the house on the west side with just a wall and a door separating the two. He had traveled back to Mobile on vacation December, 1968. Ada's grasp of what might be a problem was intensified when she received a letter from him stating the Sunday he would be returning to San Antonio. She realized it was the coming Sunday. Also, he requested that she leave the screen door unlocked when she went to church so he could enter the house. Ada pondered about her concern for a few minutes and rationalized that he would be going to work before the children arrived, and they would be picked up before he returned. And then she thought, why am I worried about this, this is my house and I can have whomever I want in it.

As she had a penchant for taking on family problems, she was now concerned about her daughter's financial status because Wee Wee shared with her that her husband, after 24 faithful and devoted years of Federal Civil Service employment was retiring March 11, 1969. This meant there would be a dip in their monthly income. But she realized that this mature son-in-law had already become an entrepreneur operating two gas stations on two corners a block from her home, and he became a "bird-dog" car salesman for Wilson Pontiac car Dealer. In fact, according to Wee Wee, he sold more cars than some of the fulltime employed salesmen. He was also studying to become a Reserve Officer for the Bexar County Sheriff's Department. In January 8, 1964 he was elevated to the Sublime Degree of Master Mason by the M. W. St. Joseph Lodge of the Grand Lodge of Ancient Tree and Accepted Masons. He was a descendent of one of the historical 52 Negro family residents of the small town of Runge, Texas.

Meditating on all this, Ada's conclusion about the matter was that her daughter's financial status she did not have to put in her "worry-about" box laughing to herself. Certainly she shouldn't have any concern because she had just bought her second Cadillac car—a 1969 gold colored Coup Deville.

Ada even allowed during this season her two cousins Gladys and Amelia from the Joiner family to come and use her living room for their courting purpose.

Ada, best defined as the altruistic one, had co-mingled her life with so many relatives and non-relatives it appeared that within every six month period someone in one or the other of the two groups was experiencing the sunset of their lives, and a celebration of life was held. May of 1969 she received a large envelop from her sister Mollie in Lexington, Texas whose enclosure was a letter and celebratory program that read "In Loving Memory of Private Dan Larkin October 29, 1896-April 26, 1969. He was her sister Mollie's only husband though estranged. Ada admired him for being the entrepreneur that he was and his devotion and care of his and Mollie's only daughter Dorothy. Dorothy lived with her father after he and her mother chose a state of separation and the fact that Mollie had a live-in significant other. Apparently they never actually divorced because Ada's reading of the program "He leaves to mourn" section listed his wife as Mollie Larkin, daughter Dorothy Mitchell, brother Obra Larkin of San Antonio, grandson Willie Vernon Woods of Guam (Dorothy's adopted son affectionately called 'Putlum') and three grandchildren. Mollie explained in her letter why she didn't call Ada. She wrote that she felt that she had too much on her hands with the grandchildren she cared for daily. Ada was grateful that she understood and immediately called her and had a long conversation about the past life of this 73-year old good man.

CHAPTER 53

The Last Season

Ada looking back at family sunsets, she was acutely aware she was in the winter season of her life's journey. Her body was beginning to let her know that changes were occurring. She was beginning to experience pain in places she hadn't before. She would occasionally say something to her daughter and older grandchildren, but they would laugh about it because her activities had not ceased. To them this did not reflect any health changes. But Ada knew it was happening although her independence never wavered. She was still taking care of her business transactions and monetary responsibilities. She felt it was necessary for her to go to the bank and deposit or withdraw money. For household or department store bills she had she was adamant about going to each establishment to pay her bills.

Things changed as a result of an almost fatal event at Commerce and Alamo Streets down town. She had been in Joskes Department Store on that corner to pay her bill. Leaving the store and stepping on the street hurriedly to cross it so that she could board the S. P. bus across the street, she didn't realize she stepped out in front of a huge city bus that started to move as she moved in its path way. Because of her height or lack of height and small statue the bus driver didn't see her. But passengers on the bus did and they started screaming causing the driver to immediately brake. He rushed out of the bus to see what he couldn't see and witnessed this tiny senior citizen still with her hand pushing the bus as if she had an impact on this action. Since this paralyzed the four corner of on-lookers and the bus on the opposite side she needed to board, the almost fatal catastrophe bus driver waved to the bus driver across the street and personally escorted Ada across the street to the bus she was trying to get to. Passersby could hear the claps of people on the bus she tried to stop from running over her.

Shook up about what could have happened that Saturday, on Monday evening when Wee Wee came to pick up the children Ada told her what had happened. From this episode her daughter realized the true station of life her mother was in. Diplomatically she described a plan that would prevent her from physically going to places to pay her bills. She was very convincing. So every month thereafter her daughter came by, paid every bill by check, and mailed them to all the companies she had balances to be paid.

This take over of her vital business actions allowed Ada to spend more time answering letters and sending gifts to the tenants who had been transferred to another base. They were the Laura and Floyd Grays in Detroit, Mary and Booker T. Jones in Oxnard, California and Willie and Dessie Austin in Creola, Alabama. They felt the need to send to her the obsequies of their young 21-year old son S/P4 Willie Austin. Willie was killed while on active duty in Viet Nam April 29, 1970. Others were Dorothy Swope (Nathaniel Bright's daughter) at Langly AFB, Virginia and all of her sister Betty's children in Houston, Texas—Isabella McFarland, Elnora Tarver, T. M. Taylor and Louisa Taylor Wilson.

Philanthropist Ada, as one might call her, did not hoard nor save a lot of money she received. She made weekly tithes/offerings to her church and gave to many. Somehow, for reasons unknown, her house became the stopping ground for weekly 'hobos' who stopped for a hot meal and a little cash to get them to a better place in their job seeking process which was questionable but Ada believed them.

Perhaps because of age, Ada had become vulnerable and less apprehensive about the intent of people who sought her help. But one cloudy day when a storm was on the radar a well-dressed Negro woman came to her house with an impressionable brief case and some hand-held-fliers. She convincingly told Ada she had some good news for her. Ada invited her in, served her coffee and a slice of her fresh baked pound cake in which she ate with visible satisfaction. With excellent diction and command of the English Language, she began telling Ada how she within a near future could increase her cash holdings. In fact whatever she had on hand she could double it. Ada was convinced but it was a blessing that she had only $25.00 cash on hand and she would not be able to go to the bank to get more because of the children. It was obvious that this grand dame was not truly satisfied with Ada's small petty cash, but she had to go on with the plan. She took the $25.00 continuing her convincing dialog with Ada. She wrapped the money in paper, placed it in a bag and placed the bag in her brief case and closed it. She asked Ada for another cup of coffee, and while Ada was in the kitchen, she did the switch in the brief case. As she continued to talk, she reached in the brief case and retrieved the bag. She gave it to Ada and instructed her that she should not open it for another hour. Shaking Ada's hand and smiling she left. Obedient as she had been instructed, Ada waited an hour before opening the bag thinking that she was going to have $50.00 or more. She had a rude awakening when she opened the bag to find shredded paper and no money. She wanted to cry, but instead she prayed briefly for the conniving woman and her deceptive act. Ada wasn't hurt for money because she was going to receive rent money from tenants the next day.

Like every day when Wee Wee came to pick up the children, she and Ada always had a brief sharing of each other's daily worthy events. Ada felt she definitely needed to tell her daughter what had happened on this day. When Wee Wee heard the story, she was livid and surprised at her mother's lack of knowledge about the 'Pigeon Dropper' circuit. And she lashed out vehemently, "Mama she was a Pigeon Dropper. I thought you knew about this city activity of these lowly predators." While continuing to talk about these despicable people who prey on senior citizens, she opened her purse, took out $25.00 and handed it to Ada. Ada wouldn't take the money explaining she had money coming the next day. As Wee Wee and the children left, Wee Wee realized she and her husband had to be more vigilant by being seen more on her property. And she made it happen. She also talked to her tenants that she knew loved her mother as if she were their kin.

CHAPTER 54

Third Generation Pride and Joy

As the year 1970 was rushing through, the Woods and Lott families were truly excited with great anticipation because Andrea Lynn White, Ada's first granddaughter, was graduating from high school. She had done very well in high school because of her talent in music and singing and her ability to type 100 words per minute and take short hand at 100 words per minute also. She had the privilege to represent her school in Dallas, Texas where she competed in the typing and shorthand competition. Not only did she compete but she was a winner bringing back to her school a first place trophy in the two areas. At home for a few days she was treated, in a laughing manner, as if she were royalty by her younger siblings. Frank, Ada's oldest grandson was making inroads in his high school studies and activities especially in his Journalism classes. He was the first African American student in the schools' Journalism discipline to serve on the staffs of all of the school's publications, and he was Editor of the sport's section of the schools monthly publication. He had a rare teenager affinity for Ada his San Antonio grandmother. Every Sunday of his three high school years he would don his Sunday best with hat, walk to Nebraska Street, take the bus and travel to Ada's house. He would have breakfast with her and go two blocks away to Greater Corinth Baptist church for Sunday-School study. Despite Ada's physical condition was no longer at it's peak healthy situation, this teenager had a very special place in Ada's heart, and she never complained about rising early every Sunday morning for three years to prepare breakfast for him and get herself ready for church. She became a non-certified counselor for the young boy who shared with her his conflict with and the treatment of his stepfather. Ada understood the motivation of Rufus and his actions. Deep inside she knew the history of his biological father Frank White's societal unlawful escapades. Observing Frank in his daily activities his discerned potential and excellent school achievement, as an over exuberant disciplinarian Rufus lacked the diplomacy to render discipline action with an "I'm proud of you" action this young boy needed. He had never been under the influence of his biological father, inasmuch as, he was only 5 months old when Rufus and his mother married. But 'old school' banked on the ideology of 'the apple doesn't fall too far from the three.' Ada realized the problem and had a way of explaining the 'why' of the stepfathers actions, but cautioned Frank to not give his stepfather any indication that he wanted to do or was doing the things his father engaged in that got him in trouble. Young Frank Jr. honored his grandmother's counsel, but didn't have to change his behavior. He confessed his faith in Christ, was baptized and was an active youth at Greater Corinth Baptist Church.

A letter written by his mother and sent in 1972 to the Express News for their solicitation for and selection of 12 Top Teenagers of the year in the San Antonio, Texas metropolitan area, Frank was one of the twelve selected and the only African American. Family, in-laws and Corinthians were elated to see the big full-page picture of the honorees and the bios that had been sent by those who submitted the letters. Frank was now truly a celebrity at home, at school and at church with a proud mother, grandmother and stepfather.

CHAPTER 55

Physical Changes Affecting Matriarch

Since Ada's dire experiences with the city SP Depot Bus, she became more cognizant about her physical problems. In fact, her falling several times was due to the deteriorating condition of her knees. Yet, she never felt the need to use a cane nor complain to her daughter or grandchildren about the pain she experienced.

The 1971 period of her grandchildren's educational success, an unforeseen bombshell did hit. Her daughter was exasperated and in shock. It was because of the granddaughter Andrea Lynn. In tears Wee Wee related to Ada how her daughter had been accepted to Prairie View University her Alma Mater, every thing that had been purchased for her first year at the university, but Lynn had changed her mind and declared that she was going to get married. Although Wee Wee was devastated by her decision, Ada thought without sharing her thought that perhaps the girl now a young adult needed to get from under the strict rule of her stepfather who had caused his own daughter to take this route of independence. Lynn's issue with her stepfather, one particular, was when she and her high school singing group composed of two girls and three boys had performed in a group singing competition in a downtown location and won first place. She was so thrilled to come home with this trophy. But because it was almost midnight she was greeted with a slap on the face, a severe reprimand and knocking the trophy out of her hand by her stepfather. This caused a real verbal confrontation between Wee Wee and her husband. But he was fast to remind her how Lynn had been caught climbing out her bedroom window to go to unknown places with teenagers she called her friends.

Ada had little to offer for the inevitable, and Wee Wee told her mother that she would spend her daughter's first year college tuition on her wedding, and when and if she decided to go to school her husband could send her. She was adamant in this as she shared with Ada the fact that she was transitioning in the massive educational manifesto of cultural equality mandated by the federal government. She had been selected as the first Black to be assigned to a counseling position in the Foundation Program at Thomas Jefferson High School the San Antonio Independent School District's largest high school. This school was considered the elite because of its location on the north side affluent predominately White community. She certainly felt she had some racial hurdles to overcome.

At the end of the day on her new job, Wee Wee still stopped by her mother's home for a brief conversation—mostly to check on her physical condition. Ada, however, discerned a slight difference in her daughter's countenance. Reluctantly she decided to delay her curiosity for at least a week. It was time, and as Wee Wee came in and sat down for their normal chat, Ada burst out with, "You haven't told me anything about your new job. Do you like it?" Wee Wee knew what the questioned entailed, and she began her sanctified opinion: "Well to start it's a distance from my home on the northwest side of town. At Riley I was three minutes from the school. Now I am 25 to 30 minutes depending on the traffic from Jefferson High School. The school was built to accommodate at least 3000 students. It's a beautiful building with three levels including a full basement. The staff and students act like it's a shrine. They love it. The interior is accented with dark wood giving a presence of darkness. I don't understand the reason for that. It's just 'dandy' that this year they are installing central heat and air in the building. I'm told it is costing as much to install these units as it cost to build the school when it was built. I am a pilgrim you know as she joked. African American faculty members are miniscule, and as Counselor in the Foundation Program, I am the only one in and administrative considered position. My second day Mr. Chambers, the principal, came by my room, took me by the arm and escorted me to the cafeteria. I was astonished to see the gathering there. The principal said, 'this is break time for some, and this is what we do.' So I witnessed coffee drinkers and donut eaters in mass. We never did this at Riley. One positive spiritual policy in the school is that at the noon hour a bell sounds and no matter where you are—walking in the hallway or in a classroom every body stands at attention for a moment of silence. Its as though time stood still for this moment of reverence to exercise whatever faith you have for praise and thanksgiving. Can you imagine 3000 youngsters honoring this policy. They do. Most of the majority Anglo faculty members I encounter are cordial, but there are a few I discern that have that give-away expression that renders the question 'How did you get here in the district's largest high school in this affluent predominately White community?' The truth of the matter is that this quick acting integration movement of children and faculty members was the result of Dr. Hitt, the superintendent's having a brother, a state congressman informing him that if he wanted federal dollars for his school he needed to do this. There's, however, one crew-cut young white teacher who has continuously made some demeaning comment about my Cadillac car at lunchtime. Today I had enough and I said to him, 'Let me tell you something. The car you see me driving is not the first Cadillac car I have owned. You see I don't have a yacht, a summer home as some of you have and boast about. I don't have a maid or cook to do all the things I do in my home as wife and mother. Incidentally, I have five children. The reason I drive a Cadillac car is because my husband who is a Civil-Service retiree and a bird dog car salesman for Wilson Pontiac Car Dealer. Having worked at the Motor Pool at Kelly AFB, and selling cars he knows about cars. He wanted me to have what he determined to be the most efficient and dependable vehicle at this time. It was his choice, not mine. Now I hope this will put your comments to rest about the car I drive." Ada, very concerned about her daughter's welfare said, "Honey you have to be careful what you say to anybody. You have no idea what he might do to you or your car because of the things you said to him." And Wee Wee fired back, "Well you sound kinda like daddy. You remember what happened to you before I was born with the old White man in the wagon that called you 'auntie' and your response about you didn't know his mother was your sister." They both laughed as Wee Wee left to go home.

She assured her mother, however, that she didn't have to worry about anything especially the wedding plans. She was going to let her friend Charles Etta McIntyre serve as wedding planner. She had given this lady seven of her graduate school written reports to plagiarize as she copied each one and submitted them as her own in a counseling course at Our Lady of the Lake University. As Wee Wee had earned the grade of "A" on each of the investigative reports so did the Wedding Planner, the Director for Lynn's wedding.

Ada had the opportunity to meet Ronald Lewis the young groom-to-be at the rehearsal dinner. She was impressed with his clean cut, handsome, debonair looks. He was a young army veteran. He enjoyed reading books and had an exemplary command of the English language which Wee Wee found to be important. As a veteran he had access to the G. I. Bill benefits for assistance in purchasing a home and higher education pursuits. Things looked promising for her granddaughter's future.

On the evening of February 12, 1971 a beautiful Wedding took place at Greater Corinth Baptist Church. Lynn Looked striking in her Victoria styled high neck, long sleeve, floor-length satin gown. Her mother was totally displeased with her choice to wear her hair in an Afro style instead of getting a permanent with a beautiful style of waves or curls.

But as the organ music continued to play long after the time the wedding was to start, panic exuded throughout the wedding party. They could not find the groom. The bride felt she had been jilted and tears began to surface on her eyelids.

It turned out that the groom was in another building calling his brother to find out where his little girl was who had been added to the wedding party as late as the day before had apparently been caught in traffic coming from the far west side. She finally arrived at the church having caused frustration by the bride, the mother of the bride and the wedding director. The director knew nothing about this last minute addition of this child as a participant. The wedding did start, and Rufus, the stepfather, gave the bride away. It was done and lives could resume normalcy.

CHAPTER 56

A New Significant Life

July 12, 1971 once again Ada was at the hospital walking the hall in anticipation of the birth of her first great grandchild. The newborn was a beautiful little girl that became another who gained special attention, love and care from Ada. She was given the name Sharreffia by Lynn her mother. The grandmother and great grandmother just called her 'Fe Fe.'

Despite the fact that Ada had been having trouble with her teeth since 1969 the problem and pain did not halt her activities of ushering in new tenants, regretting the leaving of others and being a constant pen pal for all those who had moved away. Especially was she pleased to receive letters from Frank her oldest grandson. He was now a college student at Prairie View A. and M. University. He was and exemplary student and gained the honor of being on the Dean's list every semester of his tenure. He loved his grandmother and enjoyed telling her jokes and grand school activities as the following 9/22/71letter indicated:

Dear Mama,

How are you making out? I'm doing okay, I guess. I've really had a grand social life. I got drunk three days straight after I got back, and some boys had to pack me back to the dorm, I've gotten two women pregnant, and one of them is really ugly; I mean Hurt! Her mother came after me, but I was so charming I ended up taking her to the movie. Aren't you proud of me?

Well, I haven't been drunk, those Girls weren't pregnant, and I didn't take any mother to the movies. So put superstitious information in to proper <u>perspective</u>.

Sincerely,

Papa

Ada, after the shock of the first paragraph, went into uncontrollable laughter reading the second, thinking as smart as he is he is also a 'jokester.' Looking at his signature she thought now why did we start calling him Papa?

Ada also received an abundance of airmail letters from her tenant and friend Nathaniel Bright who had journeyed to Wichita, Kansas where his daughter Dorothy and her family lived. In each letter he vowed his undying love for her—a non-reciprocal feeling by Ada. In each letter he was going to be returning as soon as funds for travel prevailed.

CHAPTER 57

A Season's Ending

Ada was a proud mother to learn of her daughter's promotion to the position of Director of Non-Certified Personnel in the Personnel Department at the San Antonio Independent School District's Central Office following her two-year position of Counselor at Thomas Jefferson High School. She was the first African American female in the position and eventually the highest-ranking African American female in the district. Her position grade was 14. The highest position grade was a 16, and that was the Superintendent's grade.

As her daughter would visit or call each day after work, Ada began telling her that things were beginning to happen to her in her body that worried her. But Wee Wee just saw her being physically fit because she hadn't stopped doing all the things she was accustomed to doing. Ada realized, however, that her tiny white pill and her garlic water were not stopping this intermittent pain in her chest. She talked to her closest friends Gussie Thompson, Mollie Mitchell and Julia Eato about what she was experiencing. All three encouraged her to see a doctor. Mollie reminded her of what had happened to Ike and her trying to take care of her three-year old granddaughter was not helping her situation. She needed to think about her age and the fact she couldn't do the same things she did thirty years ago. Their advice heightened her paranoia.

The evening of July 13, 1973 when Wee Wee made her usual visit on the way home from work Ada greeted her at the door with a facial expression that disturbed her. Her immediate question was "What's the matter Mama?" In an unusual expression she told her daughter how she was really feeling and the continuous pain in her chest. Without further dialog about her mother's physical situation, Wee Wee immediately called Dr. Melenyzer, their family physician. Dr. Melenyzer was not only a medical doctor he was also a surgeon who was altruistic in his service to Africa American patients. Wee Wee definitely had faith in his ability because he had delivered all her children and he had successfully performed surgery on a cyst that had developed just below the ear lobe of her infant son Rufus Jr. When she explained to the doctor the pain her mother was experiencing in her chest and because he knew her medical history and her age, with urgency in his voice he told her to take her to Lutheran General Hospital. The hospital was at least a twenty-five minutes drive to 701 S. Zarzamora St. on the west side of town where it was located. He also told her that he would call the hospital and alert them of her coming.

Wee Wee called her husband, relaying what the doctor had said, and that she was taking her mother to the hospital. When they arrived at the hospital, an orderly was at the entrance with a wheel chair to transport Ada to an examining room. This feisty 77-year old refused to sit in the wheel chair declaring, "I can walk, and I can walk where I need to go." Seeing her resolve, the orderly did not insist that she sit in the wheel chair even though it was hospital policy, but simply said, "Yes ma'am follow me." As Rufus walked in the waiting area to be with and support Wee Wee, Dr. Melenyzer walked in with the result of Ada's examination. She had indeed had a heart attack and needed to stay in the hospital to determine the damage and necessary treatment. It meant her eating habit had to change specifically a no-salt diet.

Well Ada became a dissatisfied patient because of the food restriction. She hated the hospital food. One day Wee Wee prepared a hamburger for her using a salt substitute. She bit into it and trashed it. The taste was not pleasing to her at all. She missed her fried pork chops and eggs, home made biscuits, homemade preserves and black coffee. Wee Wee became the senior in the room as she talked to her the second time explaining that if she wanted to get out of the hospital residence, she was going to have to eat what they served her. She was blessed that she had not passed out before coming to the hospital which would have necessitated the use of instruments to jump-start her heart. All she had to do was obey the doctor and eat the recommended foods. Ada was silent, surprised at her daughter's command. But she realized she was right, and she certainly wanted to go home where she had choice to do what she wanted to do.

Many of her neighbors, friends, church members, the pastor and his wife wanted to visit her in the hospital, but on the advice of her doctor only family members were allowed. Her daughter was diplomatic in making this known to those so desiring. She had an announcement made in the church in this regard, but solicited prayer by the members.

After twelve days in the hospital, her doctor's treatment, and the conscientious care of dedicated nurses who began to show true affection for Ada, July 25, 1973 she was discharged from the hospital. Her prayers were answered. She was going home. And as good as she was feeling, she believed she was the same Ada as before the attack. She felt she could do everything she did before going to the hospital including eating what she wanted to eat. In reality she did not understand or disbelieve the severity of her once-in-a-lifetime health episode because by the grace of God she experienced no more pain, she felt no weakness in her body and she was feeling "honky dory" her declaration of her present physical condition. During her exit conference with the doctor in the presence of her daughter he laid out specifically what she needed to do if she wanted to avoid another attack. She needed to curtail some of her non-essential activities, take her medicine on time and restrict her salt in-take in her food. Ada chuckled inwardly at his food order. She could not fathom the idea of giving up her well-seasoned pork chops, roasts, chicken and all the vegetables she prepared. And she thought, I'll have to figure out what to do about this problem. But thanks be to God, His mercy and his grace she was going home.

When she arrived at home, the first thing that caught her eye, was the stack of unopened letters she had received from former tenants. The word had somehow reached all that were out of the state of Texas. Former tenants she heard from were the Woodards and Austins in Creola Alabama, the Jones in Oxnard, California; the 'thank you' for the gift she had sent Augusta Johnson in Mobile, Alabama; the Grays in Detroit, Michigan; Nathaniel Bright and daughter Dorothy Swope in Langly AFB, Virginia and from her two remaining sisters—Mollie and Bertha and all their children who looked to Ada as the second mother in their lives. She had an abundance of 'get well' cards from church members and neighbors.

In bed as she read and read tears of joy flowed as she realized the genuine love these people had for her and how grateful they were for all the things she had done for them.

Well, she rested, curtailed her activities for a week. But, after that she became Ada Woods the person she was before the attack. Again she started cooking for everybody around her, caretaker when necessary for her great granddaughter Sharriffia who now lived with Wee Wee. She loved this little girl so much and so regretted her inability to care for the child. This was not her thinking but the opinion of her daughter and niece. Well, she just felt the God she served and prayed to had to be more powerful than any doctor that had treated her. She was feeling like her old self. She had no pain, and she resumed her garlic water drinking, and resumed her former eating habits, but with a little less salt.

CHAPTER 58

Swiftness of the Winter Season

It seemed just yesterday when Ike's nephew Joe, partially inebriated came by Ada's with his empty cane syrup bucket to get whatever great leftovers Ada had in the refrigerator that he could put in his small bucket for his lunch consumption at Randolph AFB. And now he was dead. Ada her daughter and Laura Bell his ex-wife were shocked. His mother had died and he had no other relatives that they knew of. Wee Wee and Laura Bell took matters of his burial in their hands. Laura Bell knew he had insurance and as a retired enlisted sailor he had burial privileges where her uncle Ike was buried at Fort Sam National Cemetery. It was well done—the funeral service and the burial.

Wee Wee insisted that Ada stay home from the ceremony but reminded her of the yellow copy of his "Designation of Beneficiary" he had given her, what it meant, and that she needed to submit a claim for the benefit.

Several weeks after the funeral Wee Wee asked her mother if she had submitted the claim. She hadn't. That evening after work Wee Wee came, helped her fill out the claim and mailed it. She told Ada that it would be some weeks before the claim would be honored because of the many submissions the government receives, but she should be vigilant in inspecting any unusual mail she received. Neither thought about it anymore. Her daughter's administrative job demands, and her son Frank's senior year in college and pending graduation were her focus.

Despite Ada's improved health condition—as she believed it to be, another problem loomed—her teeth. It was necessary that all had to be extracted and she would now have to have a full set of dentures. Giving his grandmother something to laugh about in her current dilemma, Frank the college grandson wrote her a letter that said in part "Mommy told me you got all your teeth pulled. Well, mine aren't costing me anything to come out." Ada chuckled at this and had such inner joy for oldest grandson Frank. He was completing his last year in college to earn a Bachelor of Arts Degree in Journalism. She was just so proud of the progress of this young man, his lifestyle and what he envisioned to be his career success.

Now the Holy Writ says, "Weeping may endure for the night, but joy comes in the morning." A few mornings after Ada's dental problems were over, as she received and sorted her mail, she separated the legitimate ones from what she considered junk mail. The junk mail was always trashed. That evening, as usual, she talked to her daughter about mail from previous tenants who always asked about her and her children. And as 'by-the-way' comment she mentioned about a strange letter that had the appearance of a different kind of junk mail. Wee Wee remembered what she had said to her mother about paying attention to anything thing that came from the federal government. Very calmly she asked Ada to let her see it if she still had it. Wee Wee knew what to expect. Inside the government communication was a $10,000.00 check—the death benefit designated for her by her husband's nephew Joe Lewis. Ada was shocked, but her daughter was relieved that the garbage had not been put out for pickup.

Did Ada go on a spending spree? No. She paid the tithes to her church and the rest she placed in a savings account making her daughter a POD on the account.

CHAPTER 59

The Quintessential Admirer

Ada's friend and profound admirer Nathaniel Bright had because of his daughter's emergency travel to Wichita, Kansas to be with her children while she was in California caring for her daughter who had undergone surgery. So, between 1974 through 1975 Ada received an abundance of letters from him. His salutations began with "My dear friend" and progressed to "My dear sweet dolling." Every letter he wrote he expressed how sorry he was about having to go to Wichita, Kansas; he wanted to come home, he wanted her to call him and he would pay for the call and all of her telephone bills. He mentioned how he missed her and her great grand baby "Fe Fe." And in his May 12, 1975 letter he explained that he did not tell her he would be back in June but he would be back July 15, and he was so sorry that she felt so bad about him. Ada had to chuckle at his apology and thinking about all his letters. She thought about Bright, as she called him, to be a good man, helpful in many ways. But romance on her part was never there. Thinking about his long stay in Wichita she laughed at the fact that she had not had to say to him and often did "You need to go wash your ass." And then she thought how he must have felt when she uttered those words when all he would say was "Awe Ms Woods." She felt guilty and would ask God to forgive her.

In addition to receiving this glorious death benefit and the joy she felt and attributed it to God's grace, there were other delights of hers this 1975-year. She was extremely joyous about her grandson Frank's graduating from college summa cum laude. As such an achieving student, he was selected by the President of the University to be sent to Ohio State University to pursue his Masters Degree in Journalism. Her grandson

Rufus Jr. a high school senior an honored athlete and Jr. High School violinist who was honored and talented enough to be one in the Youth Symphony Orchestra of San Antonio while in high school in addition to his athletic prowess. Vernon, a high school sophomore displayed artistic possibilities. And the youngest grandson David was beginning high school with great academic and athletic potential.

Despite all the good fortune and joy Ada had received this 1975 year, a cloud of sorrow loomed and it came in the call from her sister Mollie tearfully sharing that their 85-year old eldest sister Bertha had passed. The tears flowed as she thought about the passing of ten of her siblings. Only she and Mollie were the only remaining Champ and Isabel Green's children. Definitely on her mind was who would be next. Would it be Mollie or her?

As Ada traveled to Lexington, Texas not to carry food for her ailing sister but to see her transitional sleep and the last time in her life's journey this side of Jordan as a believer would say. She had joyous and sad thoughts about her big sister. She remembered when Bertha was eighteen declaring vehemently that when she married she wasn't going to have any children and laughed to herself because Bertha had 10 children. No other sibling came close to that number. Minor had two; Lena had 2; Mollie had 1; Ollie had 1 and she had 1. Seven had none and died young. Then she thought about the naivete of her big sister and she was sorrowful. Bertha never traveled from her rural home place, and no farther than the small town of Lexington. Tears began to surface on Ada's eyelids when she remembered a question Bertha asked her on one of her visits. Somehow the state of Main came up about some news item and Bertha asked, "Ada is that in Texas?" Ada's response was as if it were a plausible question for a senior Texan resident who had attended school, studied geography would be asking. But she realized the miniscule scope of her sister's life never having ventured beyond the Moab Community in which she was born, lived and died. Thinking on these things, Ada realized her big sister was a happy camper. She never saw her in her adult circumstances sad or complaining. She was happy, and that exuded in her countenance when she talked about her children, her husband, their vast farmland and cattle that provided all their needs. And she never worked outside of the home. The Green family members always wondered why of her five sons she named one Pink and one Green. But no one dared to ask her why. Ada had an inside laugh about that.

As they gathered at Bertha's home following the funeral and burial services, her children's attention went to Ada because in some manner everyone had experienced not only care and nurturing services from Ada in San Antonio but also gifts from her. Their resounding comments to Ada as she offered her departing gesture in the form of hugs to each was, "Take care of your self Aunt Ada." And "We love you and appreciate all you did for mama, and we're going to keep in touch."

As Ada was riding home in her daughter's new Cadillac Sedan Deville that had received visible scratches from its travel through thicket hangings on the road to the cemetery, she had a real crying spell. She thought about never seeing those exciting eyes Betty displayed when she talked about big city activities that she was never privileged to be a part of. Ada's consolation was, however, that Betty was a great wife, a loving mother and she enjoyed her loving circumstances. It was evident that she loved her strong, handsome husband and total provider for the family. This year they would have celebrated their 50th anniversary. The tears stopped flowing as she thought about Bertha's happy life despite never having left her birthplace.

Ada's prayer as she traveled home was one of thanksgiving to the God she served considering his provision and his protection of her and her child since the death of her husband. She was so grateful for the growth and accomplishments of her daughter, and she loved and cherished her five grandchildren and the two great granddaughters.

At home, as much as she thought about the fact that of the 12 Champ and Isabel Green's children only she and her sister Mollie—her partner in crime as children under the bridge—were the only ones left on the earthly realm. Depression and loneliness set in for a day as she thought about her husband Ike, her father, her mother and all her younger siblings. But her faith promoted action and the second day at home she got up with intent motivation to do something. She concentrated on church and her commitment for service still as an usher, active participation in the church Busy Bee Auxiliary and its Salad Tea which was a fund raising event and attending meetings of the Ideal Workers Auxiliary. And the Fred Brock Post meetings of veterans and wives of deceased veterans she planned to be more active. She also stepped up her cooking and serving everybody—family and tenants—who wanted to eat. Another big activity she took on was answering the massive letters she received from every tenant that had moved to another state seeking information about her health, her daughter and granddaughter and friends they had gained in San Antonio. One could surmise that she became the "411" agent for all her tenants that were now in other states. For example she received a letter dated August 6, 1975 from the Jones—Mary and Booker T—in Oxnard, California with Mary sharing that her mother had passed and her concern about Ada's health, her daughter, her niece Laura Bell, and grandniece Laura Louise Laura Bell's daughter. Willie Austin and Dessie Woodard referring to her as mother on their letter dated August 9, 1975 expressed joy about her health improvement even her handwriting and her gaining her weight back. And they sent money they owed Ada. A letter from Laura and Floyd Gray dated August 18, 1975 expressed their thanksgiving about Ada's health improvement. In addition they sought information about Birdie Frank's granddaughter being found dead and whether she received anything from the death of her husband Cusann Lemelle her brother the Creole hotel owner in San Antonio. Laura wanted to know if Bud got anything, but felt Lemelle's family should have gotten something. Four sequential letters from Nathaniel Bright in Wichita, Kansas continued his non-reciprocal undying love and devotion for her. And there was one from his daughter Dorothy Swope in Langley AFB Virginia expressing her gratitude for what she had done for her father and the gifts her children had received from her.

This was Ada's daily activity through 1978. She would not give into the fact that her health was failing, so her activities did not slumber. Her grandchildren and her great granddaughter were her pride and joy. She cooked for them, served as caretaker when needed, watched the news and variety shows on TV and was faithful in her devotion to church attendance and auxiliary work. This included preparing a raccoon delicacy for Reverend B.T. Alexander her pastor and his wife. Her sister Mollie had sent the dead raccoon animal through the mail.

CHAPTER 60

A Grandson's Unsuccessful Effort

As Rufus Jr. Ada's second grandson a senior at Southwest Texas University hurried out of his dorm, jumped in his car destined to get to his home in San Antonio in record time and return to the campus before nightfall. He was grateful for the beautiful Tuesday September 13 sun shiny day and that it wasn't Friday the thirteen. Traffic was light, but he was upset with himself for having to return home for some music he needed. He was lead singer in the University Band. Arriving at his parent's home on Morningview Dr., he opened the door and the phone rang. It was his grandmother's tenant Vincent White. It was not a call he expected. In a concerned voice Mr. White told him his grandmother was lying on the living room floor and she was 'cold.' Rufus immediately called his mother relaying the message, locked the house, and in less than seven minutes he was entering his grandmother's home. As a physical Education major he knew how to minister CPR and began ministering this life-saving act. As he was working for at least ten minutes, his mother entered the room. She observed her son working feverishly to revive her mother Ada. But, she knew when she walked in the room her mother was dead. On her knees pulling on her son's shoulder, she stopped his efforts embracing him and saying with teary eyes, "She's gone son." "Just know that she's in a better place where there is no more pain, no more sorrow. The God she served decided to deliver her from this world with all its pain and sorrow and give her a much deserving eternal rest in a place not made by man." Wee Wee took up the mantle knowing what had to be done. She called for the city coroner to pronounce the death and time, and she called the Lewis' Mortuary for the body to be picked up from the hospital.

She then called her pastor to establish a date for the Celebration of life service. "We must go now and prepare for the service for the celebration of the life of my mother and your beloved grandmother." Mr. White was devastated and had a great deal of compassion as he watched the actions of his altruistic landlord Ada Woods' daughter and grandson as they waited for the mortician.

The next day after consulting with her husband, Wee Wee chose the Sunset Memorial Park for her burial site instead of the Fort Sam Houston National Cemetery where her husband was buried.

CHAPTER 61

The Omega

Monday, September 17, 1979 was a beautiful day. There was not a cloud in the sky. Silence prevailed in the big black limousine as it followed the hearse traveling down Nebraska St. Cars approaching stopped in reverence of the procession. When at the intersections, halted by the command of the motorcycle police escort directing a slow pace reaching the interstate loop, Rufus noticed his wife looking back through the side windows watching a long string of cars that followed. Walter, her daughter's second husband noticed also and said, "Mrs. Lott there's 150 cars behind us." And to his wife Lynn he said, "You grandmother must have been a popular woman."

Rufus feeling the pain of his wife felt the need to break the ice by offering something that would generate laughter. "Well," he began, and his wife, daughter of the deceased wondered about what her 'home grown' serious comedian was going to say. In a quick moment he blasted out, "Well, I know what Ms. Woods would say to Mr. Bright." All started to laugh, and somebody asked, "What?" And Rufus said in a comedic manner, "Bright you need to go wash your a_ _." Rufus in the same manner said, "And this is what he would say: 'Ah! Ms Wood.'" His wife smiled thinking about her mother's 'raw' statements at times. Each passenger began to give his or her memory quirks about the deceased. This generated joyous feelings by the family.

They became silent as the hearse approached and entered the gates of the well kept Sunset Memorial Park where the last rites and burial would take place for the phenomenal 84 year old woman they loved and who had been called by many simply Ada.

The funeral cost for the beautiful Bronze Casket was $6,000.00 and the perpetual care burial and service was $663.50. Wee Wee wanted the best for her mother's burial. She deserved it.

Eighty-four years of an extraordinary life was summed up in four brief paragraphs on the front page of the September 27, 1979 issue of the San Antonio Register the weekly local African American Publication. Its' by-line was 'Final rites held for Mrs. Ada Woods,' but it had one error. It listed her age as 81 instead of 84. In the mind of many—family and friends—the question prevailed: How could such a productive life be summed up so briefly?

www.ingramcontent.com/pod-product-compliance
Lightning Source LLC
Chambersburg PA
CBHW020422290526
45785CB00002B/688